THE PASSION OF RICHARD BROWN

ABOUT THE BOOK

Richard Brown is an Irish-American who returned to Ireland in search of his roots.

With Celtic élan, he was borne away by the adventures of the moment, the strangers he met in pubs or in the street, the weird and inexplicable situations he kept stumbling into. He recounts his adventures with humour and anti-heroic candour – in the great Irish tradition of the anti-hero as observer. With this is inter-mingled an American strain of Jamesian fatalism, the Strethers who remains at bay.

The resulting portrait of Ireland and of himself is one which no Irishman or English-man, imbued in the stormy events of Ireland today, could have written. It is a compelling and dramatic story of a journey back to origins and the decision whether and to what degree to accept them into the present.

Richard Brown captures much of that Irish old-world charm which is preserved in America. It was the source of this charm, the literary, epic, heroic but gentle, halcyon Ireland that he set out to find, the eternal Ireland. Amid his inadvertent adventures with the stormy Ireland of today, he found the eternal Ireland.

GOOD READ

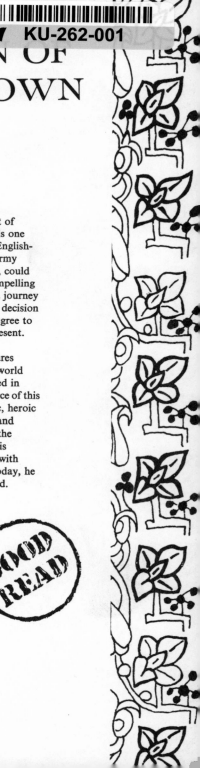

THE PASSION OF RICHARD BROWN

by Richard Howard Brown

GORDON & CREMONESI

Designed by Heather Gordon

Printed in Great Britain
by litho at The Anchor Press Ltd,
and bound by Wm Brendon & Son Ltd,
both of Tiptree, Essex

ISBN 0–86033–054–0

Gordon & Cremonesi Publishers
New River House
34 Seymour Road
London N8 0BE

There would be no book if it had not been for the more or less mad inspiration of Larry Durocher, the continuing support and encouragement of Mike and Maria Mooney, and the patience and indulgence of my wife, Violet.

Acknowledgments

Many people helped me, some in ways they're not aware of, and Frances Lindley, Dick Kluger, John Cushman, Grace Darling Griffin, Hugh Lunney, Chuck Lawliss, Carol Eron, George Wieser, Harper Barnes, Bob Rotner, Carol Rinzler, Jim and Mary Newton, Maurice Johnson, Eamon Brennan, and the Colonial Diner, were among them.

PART I

one

It was St. Patrick's night and I was standing in the lobby of the Gresham Hotel wondering where it was that Cathal Brugha had stood before he kicked his way through the big doors out into the street with a gun in each hand and made them shoot him. I was wondering where it was that he had made his decision that he would die for Ireland.

Before that I had been drinking and talking with a worn blue-suited barrister, "penurious but ambitious," in several Dublin pubs since early in the afternoon, and we had both been drunk, not badly but with that sense of discipline and dignity you get from mixing whiskey with important discourse.

It started at McDaid's. I had gone there because I'd been told it was one of the places where Brendan Behan drank and a some-time IRA hangout as well, and the IRA figured prominently in my idea of Ireland. It was crowded and noisy and above the smells of smoke and beer there was the strong smell of disinfect-ant. I stood over in the corner near the window booth, squeezed in at the bar with a large pot of soup steaming on a hot plate at my elbow. A gaunt man in an oversized overcoat that hung loose on his body asked me if I'd seen the parade. It had only lasted an

3 ·

hour and a half and I had missed it, but I wanted him to know I was Irish and I told him I had marched up Fifth Avenue in the one in New York when I was in college. He said it was too bad I hadn't seen the parade in Dublin that day because the Yank kids with their band from a high school in New Jersey or somewhere had taken all the spoils.

My idea of being in Ireland was not to watch Catholic high school bands from America, or even talk about them, and after a few minutes I asked him if it was true that the IRA hung out there. He was hunched over his glass and he ducked down even further into his overcoat and looked at my shoulder and rubbed the back of his hand across his mouth and whispered, "Watch it. The ears have walls."

I started to smile at that, but because I was a stranger, and whatever way he'd said it, it was a warning, I didn't want him to think I was laughing at him, so I looked away at the faces of the other drinkers and at the mustard-colored walls. Because it was a holiday, there were a few women and some small children in the bar, but it was mostly men, and I felt stupid and self-conscious for having asked him right out about it. It was like the night I arrived in Paris when I was twenty and I went looking for the Existentialists at the Deux Magots. I was making the IRA a tourist attraction.

A voice behind me said, "You'd better drink that up before it turns to ink," and that was how I met the barrister, a thirty-ish, snub-nosed man with curly hair and the look of an aging altar boy. He was referring to the quarter glass of Guinness I had left in front of me on the bar. "Let us give you a new beginning," and he called for two more and a couple of Jamesons as well.

His name was Keegan. Rory Thomas Patrick Keegan. He had heard me talking with the gray-faced man about the parade. He thought the parade was a joke. He thought Dublin was a joke, too. And after the gray-faced man left, and I told him about *the ears have walls* warning, he thought that was a real joke. To him the IRA was mostly out of work or down-and-out, lower-class hood-

4

lums from the cities or ignorant farm boys. The IRA was also a joke. "If Ireland's future is to be determined by the likes of them, God help us."

Even though the warning had come out cockeyed, I had taken it seriously enough to be bothered by the way he was talking, and in case anyone *was* listening, I asked him if that was the way he felt, then why did he drink in a place where they hung out.

"My dear man, the IRA and I frequently find ourselves drinking at the same public house in this charmingly grubby little city. There are times when I can hardly stand at a bar without rubbing elbows with some seedy rebel on the run from somewhere who is only too willing to tell me of his exploits. It may add a certain spice to my otherwise bland existence, but it hardly makes the IRA and its old romantic view of Ireland relevant to my life or worth my worrying about."

I bought us another stout and whiskey, even though the owner had already announced that it was closing time. It is the custom to close the bars in Dublin between two-thirty and three-thirty in the afternoon for what is called "the holy hour." "It is an expression of our guilt over being an alcoholic people," was Keegan's comment. "I am an incipient one myself and I leave it to the publicans to keep a rein on me."

'He told me it was Kevin O'Higgins, a narrowly religious man who was Minister for Justice in the first years after the war with England, who started it because he thought it was a disgrace the way Irish men never went home for their lunch but drank in the bars instead. "He was shot down, you know, and died on the sidewalk with seven bullets in him after coming out of Mass. He had his enemies, God knows, but there are those still who say it was for 'the holy hour' that he was killed."

We stood at the bar through another three or four polite calls and finally, when the room was almost empty and it was clear the owner really wanted us to leave, we went out the back door and walked through an alley into the bright afternoon sunlight and turned down Grafton Street a few blocks to Berni's, where you

5

could have a drink at the table as long as you were eating food.

It was that kind of afternoon. I like to drink and talk but I was no match for this courtroom lawyer who was out to dazzle me, an impressionable visitor to Ireland. I knew no one, had nowhere else to go, and Keegan was fun to listen to: informed, opinionated, and affected in a way I associated with certain Englishmen I knew back in New York. He should have been dressed in fine double-breasted flannel or smart tweeds, not in a shiny-sleeved blue suit with a jacket-sweater underneath.

We left Berni's and went to Mulligan's, a working man's side-street pub beyond Trinity College on the other side of the River Liffey, and I listened to him talk on Irish politics, North and South, the IRA, its history, and the revolutionary mind. Everything he said was interesting but it was as if Ireland and its ways were an embarrassment and in explaining them it was necessary to be amusingly superior. At first his wit impressed me. It was intimidating, too, because I had no means to compete, to be equally amusing, beyond the presentation of myself as another in the long line of slightly foolish American visitors seeking out his Irish heritage. But as we drank I began to feel uneasy. It was as if he were performing for me, and in so doing, trying to disassociate himself from Ireland.

"Let them stew in their own juice," is what he said about Catholics in the North expecting Southern Irishmen like him to join them in their fight. They'd chosen second-class citizenship to get the British dole rather than be Irish and poor, but with some pride, like his parents, good country people back in Roscommon. I nodded. Was that the way to look at it? I didn't know.

"If you are concerned about my indifference to the good Papish people of Belfast and Derry, know that it is but one of twenty levels of indifference that you will encounter here in Dublin. Forget your American inclination to analyze the multitudes. We are not a people to whom social psychology can be applied. Opinion is very personal here. Think in terms of individuals, not of the hundreds and the thousands." He finished off a drink. "But whoever you talk to, you are certain to hear a lot of rubbish."

When finally there was nothing more for him to explain to me, to be amusingly superior about in his shiny-sleeved blue suit and jacket-sweater, I suggested we have dinner. He looked at his watch, seemed surprised at the hour, and told me he had a theater date and would meet me afterward. I wrote the name of some after-hours club he gave me on a scrap of paper and stuffed it in my pocket, certain, though, that I would not be there, because I'd drunk my fill.

We said goodbye and see you later outside in the early dark in front of Mulligan's. He called a cab and started to duck in and then stepped back. "Don't bother meeting me. I won't be there. I've bored you enough already, I'm sure. I'm going home to bed. Go meet someone else." He ducked down and then stood straight again, not willing to leave on so self-deprecating a note. "But remember, whoever you meet in this fair city, you'll hear a lot of rubbish."

I shook his hand and told him that rubbish is all that any of us are good for anyway. We smiled at the comfort in such an observation and he got into the cab, closed the door behind him, and waved goodbye. I waved back and then I found my way to O'Connell Street and asked directions to the Gresham Hotel.

Many years ago at The Players in New York, at an Irish night with black ties and red-faced older men, I had started to sing the first few lines of "Kevin Barry," the famous rebel song from the war of independence against the British, when a fierce, gray, craggy man in a kilt, hired to play the bagpipes, had shouted at me to stop: "Kevin Barry's mother asked that that song never be sung."

It had been the end of the evening and the old man was packing up his pipes to leave. He had known the martyred Kevin Barry I was going to sing about, as I stood with friends in my tuxedo by the piano in an upstairs drawing room of a private men's club on Gramercy Park. He had been wounded with his

7

brother in the battle at the Gresham Hotel in the civil war that followed the Treaty, when Cathal Brugha refused to surrender and came out into the street with a gun in each hand and made them shoot him. So remembering that, and for Kevin Barry and his brother, and the old piper, and Cathal Brugha, too, and because it was a fine hotel and I was hungry, I set out up O'Connell Street for dinner.

In the Gresham dining room, alone in a gray jacket and slacks and sweater, my breath bad with drink, I was self-conscious and ordered soup and an expensive steak to prove my worth. The walls were covered with deep rose-colored fabric and there were old framed prints of horses and white wood trim and large white doubled doors. A group of women in long dresses and velvet pantsuits and slim, gray-haired, moneyed men waited to be seated, and I thought how they should be photographed for the fashion pages of a magazine. And still drunk, maybe not badly, but that sense of discipline and dignity clearly gone, I tried to steal the silver. It was heavy and distinctive and each piece bore a decorative "G", and because of the time when that fine hotel was scarred by shells and black with smoke, I wanted it.

It is a joke to steal a spoon or an ashtray in the company of friends and easily brought off, but alone, if there is risk, it seems a mad and irresponsible act. The fork and the knife were up under the sleeve of my sweater, the knife tip touching the metal band of my watch, when I lost my nerve. I regret that now, but that other side of me, respectable and afraid, even as I thought of civil war, made me slowly slide them out and lay them back upon the table before the waiter came to take away my plate. I drank my coffee quickly, sure that he had noticed, overtipped him, paid my bill, and left.

I went out into the lobby, which was modestly elegant with crystal chandeliers and fat black cherubs holding ornate, gold-leaf candelabra, and wondered where it was that Cathal Brugha had stood when it was a shambles fifty years before. Charles Burgess was the name he was born with, but he wanted to be

8

more Irish than that. He had been Minister of Defense during the war for independence, but when it was over, he would not recognize the treaty that divided his country North and South and demanded an oath of allegiance to an English king. Cathal Brugha was a dreamer. He wanted a republic. And when, after days of fighting, the others like him finally surrendered to the forces of the barely formed new Irish Free State, gave in to troops that had been their comrades in rebellion the year before, he would not.

Did he make the decision that he would die for Ireland there in that lobby? He had fought in Easter Week and had seen what death, self-willed and for a cause, might mean to an indifferent country. Still, was he afraid? Were his palms sweating against the pistol grips? Did he say a prayer before kicking the doors open onto O'Connell Street with his pistols blazing like a desperado?

I went out into O'Connell Street myself and the night was bright with holiday lights and girls were walking hand in hand and in groups and some with boys embraced in doorways. I smiled, remembering other nights on pass, long ago with soldier buddies, sailing up to girls like these, and I hummed old tunes and walked the whiskey off.

I turned down to the bridge past the British bullet-scarred monument to Daniel O'Connell, the great spokesman for Catholic emancipation, and then across and up the other side under the columned portico of the General Post Office and all the way to the monument to Parnell, "the uncrowned king of Ireland," whose career and life had been broken because of his love for another man's wife. The street is a broad one and there are statues honoring the less famous along the tree-lined median strip, and I crossed over and examined the one of Father Matthew, the Apostle of Temperance. I read the inscription and looked up at the granite figure in monkish robes, its right hand raised, and shook my head, enjoying the extraordinary look of Dublin, amazed that I was there.

two

My introduction to being Irish was the St. Patrick's morning when I was six years old and my mother pinned a doubled-over strip of green ribbon to my sweater before sending me off to school. I don't know if I actually remember it happening or merely think now that I remember because my mother told the story so many times over the years that the story and the incident are one, but as a little boy I was confused at having to wear anything so girlish as a ribbon on my sweater and even more confused by the news that I was Irish. Up to then I had considered myself Jewish because I had been born in New York.

In truth, I am only half Irish, and that half is removed by more than a hundred years from Irish soil. My father's family origins were proudly English. He was Presbyterian when he went to church, which has only been on a very few occasions that I know anything about, and largely indifferent to Ireland and things that are Irish. My mother was Catholic and that, in the days when I was born and growing up, was that.

The formation of an Irish identity, or perhaps better said, the identification of myself as Irish, was a gradual thing. It started with my Catholicism, an experience I shared with many, including those who were clearly more Irish than I. Though the Church was universal by definition, Jewish in its origins, medieval and European in its spirit and tradition, and Italian in its ultimate leadership, on the parish level, at least in the Archdiocese of New York in those days, it was easy to think of it as the special province of the Irish, if only because most of the priests and a great many of the laity bore Irish names. It was commonly understood that it had been the dedication of an immigrant Irish clergy that had established Catholicism in Protestant America, and this was reason to be grateful if you took your religion seriously, which I did, though in a very ordinary way, and to feel just that bit superior if you had any claim to being Irish yourself.

There is still today a large rectangular bronze plaque in the rear foyer of the church where I made my First Communion and Confirmation and on it are the names of all the men in the parish who had served in World War I. I remember one evening when I was in my late twenties, perhaps already thirty, reading through those names after Confession, keeping a comparative count of those that were Irish against all those that were not; pleased that there were more Irish than all the others put together. The time of that plaque is gone—was gone even when I was reading it—but I was enjoying it for what it said about the past. Those were the names of old men and most of them are dead now. I knew who some of them were when I was a little boy. Not many of them ever got to be important. They weren't the big benefactors who wrote out ten-thousand-dollar checks to build new altars, but it is unlikely that there would have been a church there at all if it had not been for them and their kind.

The vestiges of their time and of their parents' time remain and are reaffirmed each St. Patrick's Day for all the non-Irish to see and enjoy or be exasperated by. It is ironic that it should now be but one step removed from a national holiday in this Protestant land, for at bottom I'm sure it is more than just a jaunty, tuneful, good-time extravaganza. A modest celebration may suffice for Dublin, where assertion of religion and heritage is no longer necessary, but in a place like New York, a gigantic mid-city-paralyzing display of bands and marchers is indulged in still.

It takes five hours and more for all those Catholic high schools and colleges, Irish county associations and church groups, nurses, policemen and firemen, military reserve units, and veterans organizations to cover forty blocks, and all along the way the sidewalks are packed with people watching. What is not understood with all the cheap "Kiss Me, I'm Irish" buttons and the mottled green-dyed carnations is that it is also a trumpeting show of power and influence; a yearly reminder to all who are not Irish that the dumb Paddys who started out sleeping eight and ten to a room in slum cellars and were lucky to get a job hauling manure now ran the town, and what do you think of that?

I was a marcher once, on a windy cold gray day after the war. That was during my first two years of college at Iona with the Christian Brothers of Ireland. We were all in overcoats and green ties and most of us had a couple of drinks in us against the cold and because it was a holiday outing. It was eyes right and step smartly as we passed the Cardinal on the steps of the Cathedral, but the rest of the way we kidded with the girls behind the barriers along Fifth Avenue, calling out to them to meet us for beer when the parade was over.

I had been a public high school boy and marching on St. Patrick's Day was a treat that first year, another new experience that set me apart from what I had been. Iona was heavily Irish in those days, a small college in New Rochelle only six years old, narrowly Catholic in the old way, its student body swollen by the G.I. Bill and far too large for its limited facilities. To me, who had not been in the war, a teen-ager still, all those Boyles and Hanrahans, Dillons, Clarys, and O'Briens, in their worn Army field jackets and old Navy pea coats, and their sixty-five dollars a month from the Government, were grown men.

12

They were not all Irish, of course, but I remember them as if they were. One day over coffee at the diner across from the college there was a dispute about Ireland's neutrality, which had made it possible for German submarines to lie off its coast in wait for U.S. merchant ships on which some of my fellow students had served, and I remember this fine point impressed me because I knew nothing real about Ireland, and most of what I knew about the war I had just missed going to had to do with fighter pilots and Marine landings on South Pacific islands.

Those were the days when sex meant mortal sin and each spring all of us were gathered together in the big gym for the annual spiritual retreat, and young men who'd been away in service, who had seen other men die, who would regale each other with stories of the nights they had been "laid, re-laid, and par-laid; stewed, screwed, and tattooed" in cities and ports all over the world, looked uncomfortably at the floor when the visiting priest spoke of the body as the vessel of the Holy Spirit, a fragile, vulnerable gift from God that we so casually soiled and violated in His eyes with our lustful thoughts and impure actions.

One does not easily recover from such concepts, yet I don't think it was that I was more impressionable, a teen-ager who had never been away from home, because most of the others were from Catholic schools before the war, had been instructed since they were children by celibate models of manliness, like those Christian Brothers in their floor-length black cassocks, and knew even better than I, with only two years of parochial schooling behind me, the special intimidating nature of authority clothed in black clerical garb.

There were a few lay teachers, but the Brothers ran the college and, like school children, we all had to shuffle to our feet beside our chairs to bless ourselves and say a prayer before each class they taught. Many of the older ones spoke with brogues still, and I was told that half of them had been wanted men on the other side during the Troubles. Though I was vague then as to exactly

13

what it was the Troubles had been, and suspected that "half" was an exaggeration in any case, it was pleasing to think that some of these men in cassocks might have been outlaws once.

There was one we called "Himself," a long-jawed blond man with glasses named Concannon, who used to tell us we'd all be better off if we got down on our "benders" and said a few prayers now and again. One day he challenged a loud-mouthed veteran to go out in the hall because he was cutting up in class. That was the style of a lot of them, good guys and kidders, but willing to take you on if you got out of line.

There was a Gaelic club and a hurling club and it was the first time I had been around anything more Irish than a Holy Name Society variety show with Father Mahoney nervously singing "Mother Macree" to end the evening. Up to then I associated being Irish with the names of the people I saw at Mass; with Bing Crosby songs; with my mother's reporting a policeman's compliment on her Irish blue eyes. This was the real thing, I thought. I enjoyed being around it and talking about it, but those Irish guys were *they* to me and whatever *I* was, I was outside it still. I never joined the Gaelic Club, or even understood what hurling was about, but I was becoming more aware that being Irish Catholic was something different, and I would draw on that time in years to come and the fact that I had been part of it would mean more to me afterward than it ever did when I was there.

I left the Brothers after my sophomore year and finished school at Syracuse, an English major with serious-minded Jews for friends. I forgot about Iona, thinking it could not compare with a big university that had so many things to do, so much to learn, and so many ways to be. I read books all the time, word by word, looking for repetitions that would provide a key, and literature became a world of hidden meanings and literary criticism was more important than the books themselves.

I talked learnedly and pretentiously about those keys and secret meanings over beer and became an honor student and went

14

to Oxford for the summer. And I began to lose my faith but not the need for it. My depressions were monumental and weekends I got headaches because weekends meant Mass. Because it was easier to go than not to, I went, arriving late and standing in the back. Instead of a missal, I read from a small black leather-bound New Testament, underlining passages and looking for repetitions and keys that would make religion like a course in Western Culture.

I knew only two other Catholics in all my time at Syracuse, both Irish and local dayhops from the Tipperary Hill section of the city, where Irish kids had stoned the traffic light until the authorities finally yielded and placed the green light over the red. One was a bitter, pale-faced graduate student in philosophy who'd started out to be a priest, but by then was an atheist who carried a briefcase and always wore a tie and who knew all the Thomistic arguments but would not believe in any God that permitted what he'd seen in war. The other, with far less hurt in him, was a boozer, a white-bucked charmer and captain of the golf team. A great one for proclaiming dirty hour if a promising girl was present, he was also given to making Latin pronouncements on the moral nature of Man.

Over the years after college I always presented myself as simply a Syracuse graduate, the product of a big university that everyone has heard about, and because of that, someone to be taken seriously. But Iona, or my memory of it, better defines me. It is not so much what it really was then, but the sense of what it was supposed to be: a collective male learning experience based on the shared premise that the Catholic Church was the one true church. If that wasn't recognized by all, it was meant to be; and if some never thought on it or took it seriously, then that was their responsibility, and their loss.

Years after that time, after I was married and had three half-grown children, after I had made money and was thought by some to be important, had known success and failure I never

15

thought would happen, I met Brother Concannon, the one we'd called "Himself," on a New York street corner. After so long, there was little we had to say to one another once we were past the first pleasant surprise of recognition. I asked him how the Irish Christian Brothers were doing and he shook his head and told me they had updated and restyled the Order to express a more universal mission, and that the Irish reference was no longer used. I smiled regretfully, remembering all those brogues and those reputed "wanted men" from the time of the Troubles. Then, just as we were concluding that brief, awkward conversation, he used the words "Praise Be To God," underlining some point amusingly in that casual way that a member of the religious will sometimes do, and I, who had left the Church, had returned to it sincerely for another decade, and then left again, who had not been to Mass in years, felt like clapping him on the shoulder and hugging him to me for speaking that way still.

three

I only knew my grandfather when he was old, gray, and bald, a large quiet man with glasses and a closely trimmed white stubble moustache. He was a steel man and on those visits to his home when I was little, I'd have breakfast with him at the kitchen table before he would go to work at the mill. It was a special treat to have that early morning time set aside for me to eat shredded wheat with Grandpa and have him prepare an orange in quarters for me, making small boats by cutting off the sinewy white core along the top edge and then separating the fruit from the pointed ends of the peel.

He drank his coffee black from a cup so large that it seemed to me a bowl. Sometimes on those mornings he would draw pictures for me, just a few quick easy lines on a piece of paper, and there, surprisingly, would be a deer or a funny man in a big hat. I learned how to draw from him and as I grew older, and became something of a schoolboy artist, my mother would set aside the good things that I did to take with us on the next visit to her parents.

To me, who saw him only with the eyes of a child or a teen-ager impatient with the binds of family, my grandfather was a private person. That is my idea of him, though I don't believe we were together more than two dozen times in my life, and I was too young, even at the end, to talk with him seriously about anything. I do remember telling him apologetically that I didn't want to be a steel man; that I wanted to read books and see the world. He was sitting on a bench in front of the summer cottage he had on Lake Skaneateles and I was a twelve-year-old skimming flat stones out on the water, looking away from him, sorry that I'd said what I did. His way was quiet. He just told me that no one expected me to be a steel man, but that a man had to be responsible, and that he had also wanted to read books and go to college and travel, but there had been no choice for him when he was fifteen, and that he'd gone to work instead.

He'd been a good football player when he was young and followed the game all of his life, and when I was eight years old, he showed me how to throw a forward pass. Of the pictures that I have of him, the one that is my favorite is a cracked sepia photo from the mid-1890s mounted on cardboard that shows him as captain of a team, perhaps from the steel mill back in Canton, Ohio, where he was raised: a young man with tousled wavy hair and a big moustache in a long-sleeved striped jersey open at the neck, a melon-shaped ball held in the crook of his arm, his teammates posed casually about him.

He was Richard Sebastian Read. Both his parents were dead when that picture was taken. At twenty-one he'd been appointed superintendent of the open hearth at the Canton Steel Company, the position his father had held before his death. "Do you think you can do the job, Rich?" the head of the mill had asked. "If I can't, sir, you'll be the first to know."

He was already courting my grandmother, who was Katherine Price. Because he was responsible for raising six younger brothers and sisters, the courtship lasted almost four years and there were times when she thought it might be better to marry a man people did not think of as already a widower with a large family to support.

18

My grandmother was a small, finely featured woman then, with deep-set blue eyes, sentimental and highly strung. Throughout her life she alternated the spelling of her name as the mood struck her, changing the "K" to "C," the "I" to a "Y," and sometimes concluding with an "E," and sometimes not. She had a beautiful parlor voice and an independent spirit and persuaded her father to send her to Boston to study singing at the conservatory of music there, an adventurous undertaking for a young woman to embark upon alone in the 1890s and one that saddened my grandfather, who was afraid she'd meet some bachelor with no responsibilities.

He wrote to her often during her stay in Boston, sometimes illustrating the envelopes or the top margin of the writing paper with the same sort of little drawings that years later he drew for me, commenting on what he was doing and indicating, in a funny way, how much he missed her.

Much of what I know about my mother's family I associate with half-heard stories and random anecdotes told through the years at the dinner table at my grandparents' home in Syracuse. I remember where I always sat, at the lower end near the pantry door. Some things were said for my benefit alone, in a "Remember this, this is very interesting" sort of way, which meant it was a story that would provide additional evidence of the good stock from which I came, but much of it was just grown-up talk and reminiscences that bored me and sometimes the voices had that disconnected background sound you hear before falling off to sleep.

Many of those bits of stories and references to people long dead stayed with me and helped to create an image of the oldtime Ohio world they came from, where all those relatives and family friends they spoke of existed in my mind as figures in some period piece of Americana set against white clapboard houses and streets lined with big elm trees. The women all wore long dresses with puffed sleeves and thick hair piled on top of their heads. They baked raisin bread and johnnycakes, made sweet

19

boiled hams and potato salads, and everyone drank root beer and lemonade. The men were oldtime rollers and melters and puddlers from the steel mill, all sons of Irish and German immigrants in summer straw hats and white shirtsleeves and stiff collars, who on Sunday outings pitched horseshoes and smoked cigars. Someone played a concertina and my grandmother sang "The Harp That Once Thru' Tara's Halls" and my grandfather listened proudly but appeared to be indifferent.

My grandmother's father, Edward Price, was an Irishman from Sligo. He knew McKinley well, and before his own marriage had aspired to the hand of the girl who was to be McKinley's wife. A prominent baker's daughter named Ida Saxton, she courteously rebuffed his attentions by "giving him the mitten," a kindly ritual of rejection favored by well-bred Ohio ladies of that day.

Sometimes I'd let my mind play with the idea that as McKinley's friend, he could well have been Vice-President, and then upon McKinley's death, the President. Or because he was a machinist and part-time inventor of various locks and mechanisms for which he never troubled to take out patents, and the designer of a simple collapsible fence that he sold for a modest sum to a man who passed his yard and foresaw the larger possibilities of what was to become the playpen, I'd speculate on what might have been and imagine that we were rich and living in a big house with servants.

I'm Irish because of these people, a tenuous connection perhaps, but one that matters to me. In addition to my grandmother's father from Sligo, who came out during the Great Famine and served in the Civil War with an Ohio militia unit called "The Squirrel Hunters," and afterward married Catherine Kiley from Limerick, there was another great-grandfather, a Dubliner who was a merchant seaman with three voyages to his credit by the time he was nineteen. With the passing of years, it has turned out that he was the one who mattered to me most.

20

But it was the Sligo man, Edward Price, whom I was told of first, and that because of the Civil War and my interest in it and in soldiers, when I was in the eighth grade at St. Catharine's parochial school and studying American history. I didn't care anything about Ireland then, or about the Famine or the coffin ships that brought the Irish here in hordes, or that Edward Price had been among them, a five-year-old boy who left Ireland with his uncle in 1848.

What the family circumstances were that prompted their departure, or whether his parents were still alive or already among those dead of typhus, I don't know. His father played the violin and was a teacher, so his people were of modest means, or had been once, and not peasants evicted from some hut and left to wander destitute on the roads or die in ditches. But the distinction probably mattered little then, as those were years of terrible hunger and disease in Ireland. Sligo, in the western province of Connaught, was among the counties that suffered most and poverty touched everyone.

The saving and preparation for their trip took almost a year because few of the ship owners trafficking in emigrants provided food or sleeping quarters. Transporting the Irish to the New World in the time of the Famine was a speculative business, which meant that owners invested as little as possible and moved as many as they could crowd onto a ship. Travelers provided their own bedding and provisions and payment for the trip covered passage only and a supply of water, which on the ship my great-grandfather sailed on was down to a cup a day per person within a month because most of the casks leaked and two had previously contained vinegar and the contents were undrinkable.

There were only two stoves on deck and the cooking lines were long. When winter storms kept everyone down below, the food was eaten raw. The supplies of some of the passengers ran out early in the voyage, either through miscalculation or because portions that had been gnawed by rats had been thrown over-

21

board to feed the fish. Some families shared what they had with others but still there were fights for the food that remained and two men were killed, and the fastidiousness of the first weeks was forgotten when some of those same people who had thrown food away tried to catch the rats so they could eat them.

The ship landed in Quebec one day short of seven weeks after leaving Sligo Bay. Most of those who disembarked were weak and sickly, a sorrier lot by far than when they started. Of the four hundred who set out from Ireland with my great-grandfather, sixteen never survived to see the fabled New World that was going to change their lives. Except for the few killed in fights for food, they died of dysentery and typhus and were thrown overboard as soon as they were dead.

This part of my family's background didn't concern me at thirteen, and if I thought about it at all, I'm sure I found the poverty and passive suffering distasteful. It means something to me now because I've lived through years that have seen millions die in concentration camps. Flying to Ireland when it was early morning and we were still an hour away from land, I looked down through the cotton bars of clouds to the flat blue of the ocean. I was drinking coffee and eating pastry and some men were standing near me in the aisle singing Irish songs, and I realized that Edward Price had already been a week at sea to reach that area of blue that I could see from thirty-seven thousand feet.

At thirteen, though, it was the idea of a great-grandfather who'd been a soldier in the Civil War that I liked, though the designation "Squirrel Hunters" for the minutemen who in the fall of 1861 protected Ohio's southern border from invasion by "secheschers" hardly created an image of prowess in my mind. Not that saving Ohio mattered to me. My father's people were mostly Southern and a great-granduncle and several distant cousins had served in the Army of Tennessee on the side of the Confederacy, and they were part of history too. Being able to claim family service on both sides of my country's most traumatic conflict appealed to me. A kind of historical snobbishness was involved.

However, to have Civil War veterans in one's ancestry, including one who was Irish, was a rather esoteric claim in those years. The fathers of most of the boys I knew had been in what was still called the World War, and on rainy days we would scavenge through basement and attic trunks looking for helmets, bayonets, kit bags, and other souvenirs of what up to then had been the great American military adventure of this century. With Pearl Harbor, though, the reality of a new war dominated the newspapers and movie newsreels, providing fodder for such easily roused imaginations as ours, and past wars were forgotten.

My grandfather's father, Richard Joseph Read, was not a soldier but a merchant sailor. Because he died so young, only forty-five and unknown even to my grandmother, he was never part of the nineteenth-century Ohio world I created out of all the family conversations I heard while growing up.

There are no anecdotes about him that I know, except the story of my grandfather's elevation to his job after his death. Yet though he was remote, I was always aware of his presence as father to my grandfather. Through my grandfather, I bear his name. I wore his ring—a dark green, red-flecked bloodstone—from the time of my grandfather's death when I was eighteen until only a few years ago, when the gold became too worn around the edge to hold the stone.

It may be that in some irrational way, the two are one to me, and the romantic idea of the young Dublin seafarer complements the image of the young football player who was my grandfather and counterbalances all the sober responsibility and industriousness that characterized his life.

Or maybe it is simply because his past can be precisely placed in a house on Rathgar Avenue in Dublin that I have chosen him to justify my own desire to be Irish.

Though little was said about him when I was growing up, I

know him differently from the way I do the others. Still surviving today are four letters written to him by his mother in the 1870s when he was a young man making a start in life in this new country, the certificates of discharge that record the teen-age years he spent as a seaman on the merchant ships *Nonpareil* and *Countess of Minto,* and the Dublin house he finally left forever when he came to America in 1869.

I've known about that house since I was in high school and even daydreamed that I would some day buy it. It had been called Eagle Lodge in his time and when I heard it spoken of in my boyhood, the name made me think it was an inn or a saloon. "We used to own this bar in Ireland," is the way I'd account for my Irish ancestry to friends then. It sounded loose and carefree. I was descended from a long line of whiskey drinkers, and what could be more Irish, I thought. Respectability is no great virtue to a teen-ager.

I was not aware then of the letters my great-grandfather received from his mother in Ireland when he first came over, the letters I have now, that cautioned him to be always frugal and industrious, to be careful in his decisions, to attend Mass regularly, and above all things, to avoid strong drink. There is no evidence that he lived contrary to those standards and, to the best of my knowledge, they were passed on to his children, particularly to his oldest son, my grandfather, who never in his life drank whiskey in a public bar.

I visited that home in Dublin my great-grandfather left more than a hundred years ago, and sat talking in front of an electric heater with the present owners in the musty-smelling upstairs living room. It was late on a Saturday afternoon and turning cool, and coming up Rathgar Avenue in a cab, I recognized the house immediately from my memory of an old photograph my grandfather had. It was stark square stucco and had large rectangular windows of unpaned glass and center steps with iron railings leading to a second-floor entry. In front there was a forecourt of dirt and gravel, and walls extended from either side of the main box-like structure of the house to block the rear property from view. There was a time, and that old photograph showed it, when decorative eagles molded in concrete were centered on top of both those walls to give the house its name, but the eagles have long been lost to time and weather.

Rathgar is in the Dublin outskirts, not wholly suburban, not really city. A comfortable area for the most part, old middle class from a day when middle class meant modestly successful merchants and soliciters, responsible-sounding titles in the British Civil Service, men in banks with good positions: a smaller and thus more distinctive social grouping than it is today. These are not the red brick structures of Dublin's Georgian period that went to slum and have been renovated into smart flats and townhouses. The Rathgar homes seem all dark sand and gray—the colors of stucco, stone, and mortar—with small front gardens, forecourts, and walls; all cozy gray respectability from the mid-Victorian years.

A professor at University College Dublin, a big-bodied man named Hanley, his graying hair worn long, lives with his wife and three small children in that Rathgar house today. They were courteous and hospitable, in part because I was American, a visitor to their country, an exception to the familiar routine of daily life, but also because their attachment to the past was far more deeply grounded than my own. The house had belonged to their family for almost fifty years and they were truly interested in all that had to do with its history before their time.

They showed me through the old high-ceilinged rooms, all casual disorder, with books and picture frames and mirrors stacked against the walls, and told me of the Earl of Beauchamp, who built it as a hunting lodge when Rathgar was only fields and meadows. We went downstairs and out and through the back, past an overhanging roof and over flagstones, where two big dogs were barking, then past a gardening shed with wood and long-handled tools piled against it, to a deep stretch of lawn and

25

bushes, and beyond the trees there was a house that James Joyce had lived in as a boy.

Inside again, and upstairs in the musty living room, they brought out a sheaf of heavy documents and bills of sale for me to see, papers that accounted for the various owners of the house back to the Earl of Beauchamp. One of those large handwritten sheets, creased with the folds of a hundred and fifteen years, and, in accordance with the legal fashion and requirements of the day, detailing the various relationships of my great-grandfather's family background into the eighteenth century, was signed by *his* father, my great-*great*-grandfather, also named Richard.

I ran the side of my thumb across the signature to touch with my flesh the paper where his flesh had rested. It was remarkable that I held this document in my hands and that I was sitting in the room where men and women, some of whose names I had never heard of until that afternoon, and yet who were of my blood, had preceded me in a traceable line of life and consciousness, had sat in the gaslit evenings of another century; that finally, after all the talk about someday doing it, after all the big city streets and office buildings in another country, all the places and people I had known and things I had done that were so far removed from this house in Dublin, I was there.

We talked about our families and the past; about America and their wish to visit it; about Dublin life and academic meetings in London, where professors kidded Hanley because he was Irish, as if he lived with savages in the wilds somewhere; and about the IRA, to which no one in Ireland was indifferent.

Afterward, walking down the steps and across the gravel forecourt, I was smiling. I didn't even mind that there was a Texaco station diagonally across the street to spoil the tacky mid-Victorian gentility of the setting. A gas station across the street from the onetime hunting lodge of the Earl of Beauchamp, from the house where my great-grandfather was a boy! Walking down the street to the bus stop I kept looking back to fix the image of it in my mind: the way it was set in the gray of early evening against the trees and other houses, the sense that I had been there, because it confirmed whatever claim I had to care about this land, to identify with these Irish people.

My great-grandfather had walked those streets. He had done chores in that house behind me, played in that deep back garden, studied by gas lamp in those now-musty rooms. I pictured him reading books about sailing ships and dreaming of the sea. Why else would he have gone to it, a middle-class boy not yet seventeen? His time was not the Famine. He was born when it was over. Was he an indifferent student, then, unsure of what he wanted out of life? Those were Fenian years in Ireland, when he first shipped out in 1866. The men who dreamed of insurrection then were not the violent rustics of the agrarian secret societies, but city workers, office clerks, and shop boys. Walking to the bus, I let myself think that he had been among them, and that when the rebellion came to naught, crushed before it started because of informers, that he had run away to sea. Was it possible that young Richie Read had been a rebel on the run, a sailor for two and a half years and then a revolutionary exile to America for the rest of his life? From this respectable neighborhood? So sober and hard-working all his life in America and an oathbound Fenian rebel at seventeen?

When I was seventeen I would sit staring like a detective at those seaman's papers of his, the three certificates of discharge that accounted for thirty months of sailing to ports of call around the world. I'd read all the official small print, the brief formalities scratched in the blank spaces with the quick smudged script of a ship's master signing off a crew; and my great-grandfather's hand, quick too, and smudged, acknowledging receipt of his pay. Year of birth: 1850. Place of birth: Dublin. How many dozens of forms have I filled in like that, hardly thinking, providing simple answers to simple questions, and yet those few simple answers in his own hand are almost all that's left of him.

If only because those papers survived, that time must have

mattered to him. He must have saved them in a drawer or in a box back on some closet shelf, and maybe he came upon them over the years of his marriage, the way I do pictures from the Army or old letters from girls who were once away at college, and sat down on a high-posted bed on a Sunday, with flowered feminine patterns all around him, and read them and remembered when he was a young man, sailing to faraway places and not working in a Canton steel mill every day and raising a family of seven children in America.

I'd try to picture the ships he sailed on: *Countess of Minto* and *Nonpareil.* What did they carry? What was it like to live and work on them then? And most of all, where did they go? What were the places that he saw?

When I was seventeen, I wanted to see the world that I imagined out of books and movies, and one summer night drinking beer with a high school friend, we made a pact and swore we'd meet in Singapore in four years' time. We never did.

I thought of these things riding the double-decker bus back through the Dublin outskirts, past the high walls that line those roads, the mortar fallen away in patches from old bricks and stones; past small shops and pubs and churches; and those ordinary structures different because this was Ireland. I wished I could ask Grandpa about the man whose home I had just left, and in that chill gray early evening, looking down from the upper deck at those commonplace Irish streets that were so foreign to me, I thought of my grandfather as living still and not twenty-five years dead.

My grandparents died two months apart. My grandmother was first to go. The Saturday that she was dying, my aunts and mother persuaded my grandfather, who was seventy-two and not really well himself, to stay home and not keep any vigil by her bed or in the hospital waiting room. My mother stayed with him, trying to seem busy in the kitchen and the den, crossing through the

28

hall occasionally to go upstairs, but really to look in on her father in the living room.

It was the late fall of 1946 and the great undefeated Army team of Davis and Blanchard was playing its last game against the Navy on the radio. My grandfather would listen for a while and then turn the game off and sit there with his arms across his knees, his hands clasped in front of him, looking at the rug. He was rarely casual in his manner or attire and that day he was wearing the dark trousers to one of his business suits and a white shirt and tie and brown sweater-jacket. My mother came in during one of those times when the room was silent and encouraged him to turn the game back on, telling him there was no way he could help by worrying, and didn't he know how much my grandmother had enjoyed his liking football through the years.

The Navy quarterback was "Ribs" Baysinger and his father, who had also been a football player called "Ribs," used to date my mother in college and many times had stood there in that living room where my grandfather was sitting while my grandmother was dying in the hospital. My mother asked him if he remembered how the older "Ribs" had come over to the house on Saturday nights after a game to take her to some dance with his nose scraped or his lip puffed out. My grandfather nodded and stared through the window and across the street. My mother turned on the radio again and he tried to care that "Ribs" Baysinger's son was taking Navy down the field in a wild finish that almost beat the great undefeated Army team.

My grandfather was well thought of by steel men, particularly for a remark he had made many times in his career: "The company makes the good steel; I make the bad." He worked until the day before he died and while they were waiting for the ambulance the night he was taken to the hospital, he asked my aunt to be sure to call the mill in the morning to check on a melting formula.

He was dead before that new steel was made. I came up from college for his funeral and it was after we returned from the cemetery that I was given his ring, the one that had been his father's. Because I was only eighteen, I was made to promise that I wouldn't give it away to some girl as a token of affection during a two-month romance. I never did, but I never thought that much about the ring either, and it was not until more than twenty years later that it began to have any meaning to me.

When my grandparents died, it was a simple fact of life: everybody dies and their time had come. I wasn't touched by it, because they were old and I was young. I was quiet and serious and tried to say the right things around my mother and aunts, but their deaths didn't involve me then. I never knew them, really. They were old and I was young.

It is still a simple fact that everybody dies, but looking back I see them differently. I sense now their reality as persons other than the grandpa and grandma I visited once or twice a year and counted on to give me money for Christmas and my birthday. They are father and mother to my mother and my aunts, children to immigrant parents back in Canton, who in turn had been children too. I didn't know then that when I became a parent and talked with teen-age sons about school and sports, that I would be still a son myself; or that as a grown man, I would regret that my grandfather had been a stranger to me. At eighteen, I didn't realize that something of me would remain that age, fixed inside my head for always.

Those are my Irish forebears. The Ireland of the IRA is not a part of the heritage they provide. For all my romantic speculation on that Rathgar street, there are no Fenians among them, no rebels on the run to America, no great orators pleading for Ireland's freedom. These people who preceded me were not extraordinary. Respectable "lace-curtain Irish" in the old Ohio years, true to their Catholic faith all the days of their lives, they were indeed the good stock that my aunts and mother were so proud to be descended from.

Perhaps it is because I know nothing of the things that must have troubled them; have no sense of wild dreams or deeply held commitments that were unreasonable, other than their faith, which I'm sure to them seemed almost rational; was never told of any flaws of character or bad behavior, that the adolescent part of me is unimpressed by their virtue and dependability, their hard work and responsible self-sacrifice. That is the part which now regrets the passing of my grandfather, whom I never really knew, and daydreams sometimes of that other man before him, the young Dubliner, Richie Read, sailing out of Liverpool aboard the *Nonpareil* and bound for strange-sounding ports of call across the seas.

four

When the stolen green Ford Cortini with a hundred pounds of gelignite in the trunk was driven into Donegall Street and parked in front of the shopping arcade across from the Belfast *News Letter,* I was on the train from Dublin, looking out at the passing countryside and farmhouses and thinking that I could rent my home, leave my job and find another, move my family across the sea three thousand miles and live in Ireland for a while, where everything seemed different. It was only the first day of spring, but in Balbriggan, Drogheda, and Dundalk, the warm winds off the Gulf Stream had already made the fields as green as the end of April.

A dark-haired girl with sad gray eyes sat opposite me reading a paperback copy of *The Godfather,* and as I looked out of the window I kept stealing glances at her and finally, on some small pretext, we began to talk. When she recognized my speech as American, she nodded toward her book and asked me if it really was like that in the United States, with gangsters shooting each other in the streets. I told her that it happened all the time, but that there were twice as many people in New York as there were in all of Ireland, so you hardly noticed it. I told her there were as many people and more murdered for one reason or another each year in New York as were killed in the war in the North, but again, it was a big city. I enjoyed making New York big and bad and exciting for her, the best and the worst of all the cities. She said she'd like to see it sometime but she didn't think she'd want to live there with so many people and all that violence, and that at least the killing at home had some point to it.

After a while she turned back to *The Godfather* and I closed my eyes and wondered what it would be like to live down in Kerry by the sea. There had been an American from Chicago staying in the hotel in Dublin whom I'd had breakfast with a couple of mornings, and he lived there in a room behind an inn on the Dingle peninsula where *Ryan's Daughter* had been filmed. He had come up to Dublin for the St. Patrick's Day weekend and was wearing a suit and tie for the first time in seven months. Before that he had been in business in Rome, but his affairs had become very tangled and in the various cities of Europe there were two ex-wives and four children and some former mistresses whom he had loved more than his wives. There were also debts and some business opportunities that he was no longer capable of handling, so he'd turned his back on it all and taken what was left in his savings account and bought a ticket to Ireland.

Except for the fact that there were no women in Dingle such as he had known in Europe, he was happy for the first time in many years. His room behind the inn was next to a small barn and a cow was tethered in a stall on the other side of the wall from his bed, and he said that over the months he had come to feel very close to the cow. He could hear its heavy breathing and movements about the stall at night and he was beginning to feel love for it as another living being that shared a point in time with him.

I laughed at what he said about the cow, but the more he told me about it and about sitting by turf fires and visiting each day with farmers and their wives and walking the country lanes and watching the ocean waves crash against the rocks, sending up huge sheets of spray, the water swirling up and around and changing colors, the more I could see it his way that all the movement he had known in life was right there in Dingle whenever he wanted to look at it, and it all began to sound good to me, too.

I enjoyed listening to him because he had made one of those wild, open-ended, life-changing decisions that a lot of people sometimes think they'd like to make, but I suspected he was living through some sort of breakdown and I shouldn't have been surprised at his reaction when I asked him to come to Belfast with me. We were sitting over coffee in the dining room and he pushed back from the table and shook his head several times and there was something like real fear on his face. He said there were too many things inside him that he could barely cope with and he could not handle the things he had heard about in Northern Ireland. "You're inquisitive," he said. "I'm not. Go if you want to, but I can't."

I dozed and thought I was in Dingle and we were well past the border when I awoke and I didn't realize we were in the North until I saw the graffiti—REBELS BEWARE! NO IRA HERE! FUCK THE POPE!—on the brick-walled backs of Protestant houses and factories as we approached the Belfast outskirts. As soon as we were standing in the station, a porter, a sunken-cheeked old man in a blue work shirt and one of those black leather-brimmed hats that seamen wear, boarded the train and came down the aisle, wild-eyed, leaning into seats with the news of the explosion. I couldn't understand his old man's thick accent and I thought he was telling me of a place to go like some Paris pimp with dirty postcards. Again he said it: "There's dead all over Donegall Street," and moved on down the aisle.

The first phone call had come at quarter to twelve, advising a business firm on nearby Church Street that there was a big bomb on its premises. It was common practice for both wings of the IRA to give advance warning and to acknowledge responsibility afterward if a bombing was their doing. At that time the Officials were still bombing, though more selectively than the Provisionals, and it was important to both that the public knew where to assign credit or blame. The warnings were sometimes not reliable because the fuses in the bombs did not always function properly.

There was a second call seven minutes later which, the police said, also reported a bomb on Church Street. The police claimed it was not until eleven fifty-five that they were notified of a bomb in a building on lower Donegall Street, and by that time the street itself was filled with people evacuating stores and offices in the Church Street area.

Because bombings were almost a daily happening then in Belfast, and hardly a block was not marred in some way, scares occured frequently. Many of those who mingled with Donegall Street shoppers that day must have had the same impatient "here we go again" attitude I saw in the days after, watching people crowd curiously across from some bank or department store, not fifty yards from where a bomb was thought to be. Some were uneasy, I'm sure, but others undoubtedly welcomed the sense of excitement and the relief from office boredom.

The last warning was still vague, according to the police, and there was almost no time to act on it or do anything about clearing the sidewalks because three minutes later the green Ford Cortini exploded.

Two policemen were approaching it when it went up and the blast tore their bodies apart. Most of a garbageman who had just returned an ash can to the curb in front of the car was blown over his truck. The heavy truck itself came apart in huge twisted pieces, killing two other garbage workers who were in the cab. A salesman driving through the street on his way to an appointment was killed instantly and a crowded bus, caught in the jam of people on the street, was mangled. Blood and smoke were everywhere and then people began screaming.

That had all happened before I told the girl on the train about the gangsters shooting each other in New York. After the old man had passed through our car and gone on to the next one with his news of the explosion, we left the train, passed through the customs check, and walked out together on to the station plaza facing Great Victoria Street. It was she who suggested the Europa, the modern concave-fronted hotel adjacent to the railroad station. It was convenient and perhaps she thought its newness and elaborate security precautions would make it more impregnable to IRA attack, and thus a safer place to stay.

There were attached metal fences across the front and around the sides of the hotel. Just in from the sidewalk I was stopped at a temporary wooden shack, the kind you see on construction sites, where they searched my luggage and frisked me from thigh to armpit and across the back before I was able to proceed up the curved driveway that had been converted into a maze of metal stanchions leading to the main revolving door of the hotel itself. A bellboy unlocked the door and locked it again as soon as I was in the lobby.

I had a whiskey in the grill, which was crowded and noisy still with lunching businessmen, although six blocks away on Donegall Street they had not yet finished lifting bodies into trucks and ambulances. I felt guilty and irresponsible for not being where that was happening. I had come to Belfast because it was where the trouble was; because people were killed there every day. I had no ties to Northern Ireland. The dreary Protestant city of Belfast, which was to remind me of Albany, satisfied no inner need of mine, except that the IRA was waging a war there. But the war that day had happened on Donegall Street, and I was afraid of what I would see. It was like the magnetic draw that a highway accident has when you're driving by it, and I was fighting not to look. I ordered a sandwich and a cup of coffee, checked into my room, took a shower, and changed my clothes.

36

They had cleared the bodies and the wreckage by the time I found my way there in the late afternoon. The firemen had hosed the blood away and a work force of carpenters was nailing sheets of plywood across the dozens of blown-out storefronts and open doorways and up and down the street there was the grating sound of broken glass being swept and shoveled into piles that looked like gravel.

A stationery store was open and people were buying cigarettes and candy while workmen boarded up the empty windows. I asked the proprietor what had happened. His eyes were still glazed and he told me that when the garbageman had blown over the truck, his boots, with the feet and lower shins still in them, lay like two overturned containers emptying his blood onto the street where he had been standing; that even with all the ambulances from Belfast's four main hospitals, and ambulance trucks from the Army, there still were not enough stretchers and the ambulance men and paratroopers had used tarpaulins to carry away the injured, and that they'd also used the tarpaulins to wrap the larger pieces of bodies, while the smaller portions, the hands and fingers and bits of flesh, were gathered up in plastic bags.

The proprietor was an alcoholic, away from whiskey only eleven months, and that day he'd helped move torn bodies and had guided hysterical office girls to the room behind his store so they wouldn't have to look any more at what it was like out on the street. He had not yet had a drink but he was frightened that he would not be able to survive the night ahead without one.

"What kind of an animal could have done this thing?" he asked me. "How can he face himself and pretend that he's a hero for any cause? Who will he ever be able to tell that he did this?"

I went outside again and watched the young men sweeping up the glass. It was Monday and the business day was ending and people who had been at work were beginning to pass normally through the street on their homeward route as if the bombing had never happened. A bus drove through, then an Army jeep and two cars, then, slowly, a tank. I walked up to the Cathedral Church of St. Anne at the end of the street and stood at the foot of the steps, thinking crazily, and with no memory of the outrages committed in the cause of religion throughout history, that it was wrong that there had been such horror so close to a church; that it was somehow improper, more than that, a desecration, and that greater respect should have been shown for life so near the temple of the God these Christian adversaries were supposed to worship.

There was no mark of the explosion on the church and I walked the few yards to the first building with windows shattered. There was a lumber office on the ground floor. I started to count my steps until I came to a building with no visible signs of damage. There were two hundred and forty-eight. I crossed the street and walked back up, this time passing the arcade where the bomb had gone off. The concrete facing around the entryway and the adjacent building fronts had been blasted away and parts of the girders and internal metal mesh supports showed through as if some huge tool had hacked and gouged the masonry. On the other side of the street, the hollowed-out remains of a large two-sided clock projected out over a balcony above the entrance to the *News Letter*. The steel hands were still attached to the remnants of its inner works and they just missed marking noon in empty space.

There were two hundred and forty-three steps when I'd finished walking to the end of the street near the church. I had probably lost my count passing the wrecked arcade and the debris that lay in front of it that second time, but the totals were close enough. My stride was somewhat short of a yard and therefore the shattering effects of the explosion, at least in terms of blown-out windows, had extended for more than a hundred yards on either side of the car. I calculated that a sprinter would take just over twenty seconds to cover that distance, which had nothing to do with the torn bodies and the mangled garbage

38

truck and bus, or the flying glass that had cut like a hatchet. All that had happened simultaneously. Measuring horror in terms of the space it had occupied was a way of accounting for the fact that I was there.

That night after a late dinner I drank expensively with some television newsmen and a BBC man I'd met in Dublin. We sat in the large, softly lit private bar and lounge on the Europa's mezzanine floor, all comfortable low chairs and sofas aligned in squares, and I looked out through curtained plate glass windows at the patroling armored cars and tanks on the street below. There was a dispute over which bars were safe and which were going to go up one night soon for sure, and I thought of the movie *Dead End* with the rich apartment house at the very edge of the slums and the dock where the gang of poor kids played. My room was in the hotel's rear and from it I could see the concentration of chimneys and occasional lights in the Catholic ghetto on the Falls Road only a few hundred yards away.

The two television men, one a news director, a big man with protruding eyes, and the other a bearded newscaster for one of the British services, had closed the pubs and were finishing off the night in the Europa, where guests could drink until breakfast if they wanted to, and where they were sure to find other newsmen, who were almost the only people who visited Belfast any more.

The news director said he had laughed when he knew he had to put together five minutes on Donegall Street for the evening's newscast. "I bloody well did, I can tell you. My horror threshold has disappeared entirely." Because there had been more than two hours' worth of film to edit, and because ninety seconds of the five minutes alloted to the bombing had to be given over to interviews with the Chief of Police and a Government Minister, "both of them talking shit," he hadn't had time to do anything about the other two explosions where no one was killed, or the British soldier who had been shot that day in Derry.

The BBC man said to stop Bogarting it, that the moral depravity of the people who had placed the bomb was beyond comprehension. The news director told him to come off the righteous indignation. "Any one of us at this table could have placed that bomb and you know it." The BBC man said that he certainly couldn't have done it.

"Don't give me that. It's a simple matter of disassociation. You don't even have to be a member of anything. We've all of us been indifferent to suffering and death a thousand times over."

While the BBC man argued that there was a distinction between indifference to an existent state and being the direct cause of that state, I remembered once when I was a boy placing a small flat stone on the railroad track across the golf course from where I lived. We used to do that with pennies and the next day they would be lying between the ties, misshapen and as thin as razor blades. I hadn't thought of that time in all my years as an adult. Why had I put a stone there? Had I lain in bed that night frightened that I would hear a train tumble down the embankment, and if it had, that they would find out I had been the cause? I couldn't remember.

The news director was saying, "All you care about is that it wasn't you, and don't tell me different. What are you going to give me, stories about the sorrowing wives and mothers and the little kiddies at home? Can't you see that nobody really cares?"

The BBC man was sober and this man wasn't, so allowances had to be made. Still I resented his badgering, even though it wasn't directed at me. Just walking through that street had made me feel uneasy all evening. I was afraid of sudden shattering calamities where all the little strengths of mind and character, built up and cultivated for a lifetime, might prove useless. It wasn't only that one could be killed or maimed in a moment; one's sense of person could be undone as easily.

"You mean you don't care about this," I said, folding out from an inside page of the evening paper a photo that had haunted me and handing it across the cocktail table. It showed an old man

40

with his leg blown off. A soldier was trying to comfort him but the old man was in shock and he didn't know the leg was gone. The photo had been shot head on and you saw the torn trouser leg and the stump and the blood spreading on the sidewalk. The news director hardly looked at it. He threw it back at me and it fell on the carpet. "I couldn't give fuck all," he said.

Perhaps to cover for his friend's rudeness, the bearded newscaster with the tinted glasses asked me why I cared. The news director interrupted and said he hoped I didn't think there was a simple solution sitting there in the middle somewhere between the Orange and the Green, if only people would see it. When he talked it was as if he spoke in waves because his body and head moved forward and back and his eyes seemed to protrude more with each new sentence. I shrugged and told them I didn't know, and that I was numb with impressions that were not new to them any more and that I was having a great deal of difficulty knowing what was important and what wasn't, and that my past kept coming in on top of those new impressions, muddying them still further. I told them that walking back from Donegall Street I kept thinking about the Christmas week back home when the showroom and offices of an automobile dealer I knew had blown up in a chemical fire, and I had felt that same vague, uneasy frightened vulnerability that I felt now, and that the feeling had stayed with me all night and the next day, and that I had remembered the automobile dealer running a sensational anchor leg in a relay race many years ago when we were both in high school.

"Was it a big explosion, tell us," the man in the tinted glasses asked, and the other one started to laugh, and I felt like a fool for telling such a story; as if they would care about an ordinary accident that had happened in another country.

A group of English and European journalists came upstairs noisily and joined us. There were five men and two women and they were all tight. One of the women sat on the side of a sofa and let herself fall back onto the cushions with her legs kicking over the arm. "God, I'm tired," she said. "I've absolutely had it."

"Where the hell is the waiter" one of the journalists asked us. The BBC man told him he was back getting us drinks. "Well he can bloody well get us a round as well."

"One round at least," another of them said.

"My God, you'd think they could at least put two men on at night. We've come here and saved their bloody country for them and you can't even get a bloody drink."

five

The idea of the old IRA of Seán Treacy and Michael Collins, Dan Breen and Tom Barry, might still have been one that a boy would fantasize about in the Irish neighborhoods of Queens and the Bronx, in Brooklyn, or in Boston and Chicago, but it was no fabled band of trenchcoated rebels to me when I was growing into adolescence in the essentially Protestant environs of Westchester in the early nineteen forties. I hardly knew about it. Cavalry troopers and western desperadoes, Foreign Legionnaires, even, and deep sea sailors provided the romantic sustenance on which my imagination fed when I was twelve and fourteen.

I think Mac Smyth's father was the only real Irish person I knew until I went to college. The others were people with Irish names, most of whom I knew from church or St. Catharine's, the parochial school I attended for seventh and eighth grade.

Mr. Smyth was a jaunty small man with a marked brogue, one of those people who was fun to listen to because of the way he talked; not just the brogue, but the way he used words and the way he saw things. I liked him best of all my friends' fathers. He was always kidding us and telling us stories and one that I remember best I used to suspect was untrue and only when I was much older did I come to think it might well have happened. It was about the IRA.

Mr. Smyth used to call his son and me a couple of bozos and he'd tell us that when he wasn't much older than we were, he'd been a runner for a flying column and not sitting around the house listening to the radio and wondering what to do with himself. One day he showed us where he'd been wounded by the Black and Tans. Neither Mac nor I knew what the IRA or Black and Tans were, but clearly they meant fighting and excitement, and when he lifted up his trouser leg and pulled down his sock and there, low on the back on his calf, was a half-inch indentation of scar tissue, we were impressed.

Because it was the kind of story men tell to entertain young boys, and because Mr. Smyth almost never said anything without making you want to smile, I was never sure about that wound. I accepted that it came from an Irish boyhood, but that he had been a military courier, I doubted. I wanted him to have been one, because I liked him so much, and it was not an unreasonable possibility, but it seemed improbable that any father of a friend of mine would have been shot under such circumstances. It might just as well have been the work of a pirate's sword. Still, I never let on to Mac that I had any reservations about his father's truthfulness or courage, and I was as interested as he was to see that scar again and listen to the story about Ireland and the Black and Tans shooting at Mr. Smyth as he ran through the fields to the woods where the IRA was hiding.

After the Smyths moved, I didn't hear or think anything more about Irish rebels until after the war when I was in college with the Christian Brothers. Ironically, my introduction to someone who had actually fought with the IRA came through my own father, the Anglo-Saxon Presbyterian. He had been away in the war from the time I got out of the eighth grade until I was a senior in high school, so in my college years we were still finding our way to a new kind of relationship that would account for the changes in me, no longer a boy, and a father I had known only through letters for more than three years.

We used to go to track meets together or watch indoor polo, and sometimes I'd meet him after work and we'd just have drinks and dinner at Reilly's Tavern, a restaurant and bar on West 52nd Street. In those days that street was famous, a long gaudy block between Fifth and Sixth Avenues, crowded with jazz clubs and strip joints, and to me an incongruous location for Mr. Reilly's restaurant, with his son a priest and he himself a very respectable old gentleman who didn't allow single women in his bar or tolerate profane language or unseemly conduct. It had been a favorite haunt of my father's from the Depression years, when you could get a good meal for fifty-five cents and drinks were a quarter and every third one was on the house. There was a cage with two canaries in it in the window and musicians and comics from the dozen or so clubs that lined the street did their drinking there between acts or between jobs because it was reputed to be the only place on the block besides the 21 Club that used clean glasses.

It was Pat, one of Mr. Reilly's bartenders, a large, round-faced man with dark hair combed straight back, who was supposed to have commanded a flying column for the Irish Republican Army. Strictly speaking, this was only rumor and was never established as fact by anything he said to us. My father had heard it from one of the other bartenders, or perhaps from Mr. Reilly, back before the war, and it was not the sort of information he would ever try to corroborate with Pat himself. That was my father's way: a gentleman minded his own business and didn't ask questions about another man's past if he thought they might be embarrassing. Also, though he never said it, I'm sure he saw the IRA as more disreputable than not, and therefore assumed that any former connection Pat might have had with it was not something he would care to talk about.

Whether or not Pat was ever IRA in the old days was of little importance, really. It is just that I remember him as part of those years with my father, one of the characters in a rite of passage

45

I still value. Because he knew my father as a longtime customer, he always joined politely in our conversations if business was slow, standing there at the bar with his big hands spread out in front of him, recalling Depression times and the people they both knew then, or the St. Patrick's Days when Mr. Reilly's rules of conduct were not so strictly applied because the bar was packed three and four deep from lunchtime on and not too many drinks were paid for. He was one of several men I met with my father whose lives were different from the lives of men I'd known up to then: men who didn't fit in, who kicked around on their own, wrote plays that were always going to be produced but never were, trained horses for the rich, or worked in department stores between acting jobs. There were probably bartenders around New York by the dozens then who were oldtime IRA and who would have been only too willing to talk about it, but I didn't know them. The only one I knew was Pat, and the very fact that he had been created for me as a man whose past could not be talked about made the idea of him and the IRA all the more fascinating.

Eddie Barton was IRA in the here and now, a Belfast Provisional who had been in on the Donegall Street bombing. He hadn't driven the car or made the phone calls, and he probably wasn't the one who ordered it, but he was in the command structure that did and he knew about it. Eddie Barton was a revolutionary who could accept the necessity of horror in the streets if it helped to create a new Ireland.

I met him at a benefit party on a Sunday night in New York City. I was not involved with any of the groups that were active in support of the Catholic cause in Northern Ireland, but because I had been to Belfast, an Irish restaurant owner I'd known casually for several years thought I might enjoy talking to some people from Belfast who were going to be there. Eddie Barton was to be the guest of honor.

Most of the people at the party knew one another and had

46

marched together over the months with other Irish political organizations on various picket lines. Some of them had been IRA back in Ireland, or were the American sons and daughters of fathers who had fought in the Tan war. What was happening now in Northern Ireland was the first time in years the IRA was to be taken seriously by anyone other than themselves or those like them whose political principles went back to Pádraic Pearse's reading of the Proclamation of the Irish Republic to launch the Easter Rising of 1916.

There was some dancing in the large back room to a trio wearing metallic green dinner jackets with black lapels, but more couples remained seated at the tables than were on the floor and there was still that formal air of a special night out. Most of the people were in the front room where the bar was. Except for my restaurant friend, Joe Houlihan, I knew nobody, but because he felt responsible for me that night, he went out of his way to introduce me around, saying that I had recently been to Ireland and to Belfast. That aroused some curiosity for a while because the Belfast group had not yet arrived and a good many of them, even the Irish born, had never been to Northern Ireland. But this was the early part of the evening when conversations with strangers run down easily. Everyone was polite but once it was realized that I hadn't done anything in Belfast and had merely been an observer, there was nothing much else for us to talk about, so I stood around and looked at my watch and at the door, as if I were waiting for friends, and whenever Houlihan saw me alone he introduced me to someone else.

After I had finished the first drink that my ticket entitled me to and bought a second and was standing back along the wall opposite the bar, looking at the placards celebrating the IRA and denouncing British rule, a friendly older man in his fifties came over to me through the crowd and asked who I was and how I came to be there. He was from Mayo, a big-bellied carpenter with thick, blunt-fingered hands, and he'd come out to America after the war. It was all very chatty and I appreciated that someone

47

there was going out of his way to have a conversation with me.

He asked me if I'd gone to Mass that morning. I lied and told him that I had because I knew everyone there must be Catholic, practicing or not, and I was already outsider enough not to risk placing myself among the latter. He said it had been a terrible night for him the night before, a wedding reception that had gone on very late, and that he'd only made it to the twelve forty-five with the help of God and a nagging wife. We agreed that a man needed a nagging wife if he was to stay on the straight and narrow, and we talked about de Valera and how you had to admire him even if you didn't like his politics, because he received Communion every morning. Then he just came right out with it. "You don't belong here, do you? I mean you're not in this with us, are you?"

I told him I didn't know where I stood exactly but I was for Ireland and I'd been there and that I was a friend of Houlihan's.

"And what was it you were doing in Ireland?"

I told him about my great-grandfather's house in Dublin and that I'd been in Belfast and that I was very interested in what was happening. He agreed that it was all very interesting. He nodded toward the big back room, which was beginning to fill up, and in the same chatty tone, he asked me if I knew that the IRA was a very tough bunch. I told him I certainly did. Then he looked down at his glass. "Well I've drunk this one dry," and started to shoulder his way to the bar. After a couple of steps he turned back to me. "You heard what it was that I said, didn't you?"

When Eddie Barton and the Belfast group arrived, there was a sudden change in the sound of conversation around me, a quickening and a turning of heads as Barton worked his way in from the door, shaking hands along the bar. He was a medium-sized man with short wavy brown hair parted neatly on a high forehead and enough show of sideburns to be in fashion. In his summer sports jacket, striped tie, and gray trousers, he wouldn't have been out of place on a country club terrace with Japanese lanterns and a dance band playing in the background.

48

Barton and his crowd joined the people in the back room and the trio played "Kelly the Boy from Killan" to honor him. A woman sang the traditional rebel songs, "The Bold Fenian Men" and "Father Murphy of the County Wexford," to piano accompaniment during the break and then three or four men shouted for quiet and a portly, sandy-haired man came to the center of the dance floor. He made a brief speech and said that even though the United States seemed to have forgotten all the Irish who had fought in her wars, and was choosing to stand by England, only President Nixon could bring about a settlement in Northern Ireland and we should all pray that he would intervene and, if necessary, get down on our knees and beg him to do so. Then he called Eddie Barton up beside him and introduced him as one of the most dedicated and courageous fighters for Ireland that there was anywhere today.

Most of us were crowded into the back room by then. I expected Barton to accept the compliment graciously and say a few words about the needy children of Belfast or something like that. It may have been that I was more intimidated by the idea of law than I knew, or that this wasn't Belfast but New York, or that when I had left my home only a few hours before, one of my sons was watching the second game of a Yankee doubleheader on television and the other was across the street in a neighbor's blacktop driveway shooting baskets, but I still didn't appreciate that these people had come to hear about guns and fighting and not about the social and economic problems of Northern Ireland.

Once he started to talk, there was no doubting what Barton was about. He spoke well and fervently, with that peculiar Northern Irish accent that is more Scots burr than brogue, saying there were braver people than he back in Belfast that minute, and in the internment camp at Long Kesh; men who had risked their lives each day that he had been enjoying American hospitality. These were his comrades and if he wasn't to let them down, he had to come back to Ireland with money for the guns they needed to carry on the struggle.

49

The time to create a new Ireland was now, he said. The Protestant Unionists were on the run and England was ready to throw in the towel. He told us not to listen to the handwringers who cried for peace, because the kind of peace they wanted would leave the Six Counties under British rule with a few sops thrown to the Catholics to keep them quiet. Well a few sops were no longer enough. Ulster was Ireland. Let the Protestants worry about negotiating for *their* rights. People said that in their hearts the Irish liked to lose. Well, God willing, not this time. With our help, the Provisional IRA was taking the Six Counties back.

There was loud applause and shouts of "IRA all the way" and "Up the rebels" and "Go get 'em, Eddie," and I applauded with everyone else. The trio played "Kelly the Boy from Killan" again until he got back to his table and then broke into "How Much Is That Doggie in the Window?" and this time the floor was crowded with dancers.

Barton was standing talking with some admirers and Houlihan was with him and he called me over to meet him. We shook hands and his hand was broad and thick. I told him it had been a fine speech and he thanked me and Houlihan said I'd been in Belfast and then he left us and Eddie Barton and I were alone at the edge of the dance floor, apart from the others.

His country club look was for a distance of a couple of dozen feet or so. Up close he was tough Irish with a broken nose that was scarred alongside the bridge. He was my age at least, but if you were told he was thirty, you'd believe that, too, because he was a natural middleweight with one of those hard, high-cheek-boned faces that can hold together for a lifetime. His eyes were deep-set and pale blue and his skin seemed almost white. When his mouth smiled, nothing happened to his eyes.

To pretend to myself that I was part of what was going on I asked Barton if there had been a mix-up on the Donegall Street bombing. I had heard that the first phone call had been an error, that the caller had mistaken Church Street for the street the church was on, but that the second call was supposed to have

50

been right and that the police or the soldiers had failed to act correctly on the information and had said there was a third call as part of their coverup. Was that so, I asked him, as if my presence on Donegall Street that afternoon, pacing off the yards through the litter of broken glass hours after the explosion, counted for something.

Barton said there was no foul-up, at least not with the IRA. He asked me for a piece of paper and a pencil and drew a crude map of Donegall Street and the arcade in front of where the bomb had gone off. I pointed to where the Cathedral Church of St. Anne would have been located on his map so he'd know I'd been there. He nodded impatiently and said the first call was a mistake but that the police were told the second time that the car was right outside the arcade and they were the ones who had fouled it up.

"Did you ever think that the Army might just have let it happen?" he asked me. "Did you ever think that they might try to discredit the IRA by letting Irish people die?"

I told him I hadn't thought of that, but that I guessed it was possible.

"You'd be surprised at what's possible."

As far as I knew, the bomb had exploded six minutes after the second call and within fifteen minutes of the first, which would have been short lead time in any case, but I was afraid to ask him about that and I let it go and thanked him for clarifying the matter for me.

During the next break a woman moved through the crowd selling raffle tickets, three for a dollar, on a basket of liquor displayed on a table at the back of the room. I bought two dollars' worth, hopeful that I'd win the whiskey, but mainly to show my good will toward the cause. There were some more songs of the old rebellions and a man sang IRA songs and I met a balding man with glasses who was a high school teacher and we talked about the Irish as a people like the Jews with a sense of past, and about the many instances of resistance against English rule over eight centuries.

51

The trio was playing "Men Behind the Wire," which tells about the British Army internment raids in Belfast. It is a stirring song about armored cars and tanks and guns and soldiers kicking in doors and beating up IRA suspects in front of their families and dragging them off to interrogation centers and then to Long Kesh. The chorus says that every man will stand behind the men behind the wire and the leader of the trio in the metallic green dinner jackets with the black lapels sang the chorus over and over and shook a tambourine. Most of the people on the floor were doing lindy hops and breaks and others, older, were bouncing awkwardly with pumping arms. Some of the women were dancing together, not only the fat and unattractive ones, but pretty young girls and middle-aged married women whose husbands preferred to drink at their tables and talk with other men.

The schoolteacher and I were standing by the table where the cold cuts and potato salad had been laid out and a brunette in a green slack suit and with a broad green band in her hair came over and picked up one of the four or five deviled eggs left on a tray and stood eating it there at the table beside us. I had noticed her only a few minutes before and because I was feeling so pleased with myself, so informed and knowledgeable talking about Ireland's history, I thought she might have come over to check me out, the interesting stranger in the navy blue blazer with the brass buttons. I made a remark to her about the deviled eggs and how that would teach her not to be late for supper next time.

She looked me in the face and took her time munching on the egg and then washed it down with a sip from her drink. She was a very attractive girl. I was right that she was there beside us on the chance that I would talk to her but not for the reason I thought.

"There are people here who say you're an awful phony."

It was said so simply that I didn't realize at first that her words were demeaning to me. I asked her what she meant, embarrassed

52

that she had spoken that way of me in front of another person. She took a second deviled egg and shrugged her shoulders. "That's just what some people say."

I told her I hadn't said I was anything that I was not and asked her why anyone would call me a phony.

"I don't know what you said. I'm just telling you what someone told me."

There was a tap on my shoulder and a beefy blond man with his tie undone asked me my name. I told him and he said there was a phone call for me up front. I was so concerned about what she'd said that I didn't realize that I was being maneuvered away in the classic comedy manner until I was at the bar. Houlihan was there and he asked me if I was enjoying myself. I told him it was a really good party and very interesting and I ordered a beer. In another ten minutes the girl came out to go to the ladies room and I moved in front of her.

"I can't talk to you. He's really terribly mad at you." She moved her head that little bit to indicate the back room and I looked through the crowd of dancers to where the man who had told me about the telephone call was sitting at a table. Eddie Barton was sitting with him and they were both staring at us.

"But why?"

"I don't know. But take my advice and don't go around asking questions about the Provos. They don't like it."

"What am I asking? I don't want to know their secrets." I didn't get any further because Barton was suddenly there beside me and he was the one who was mad at me.

"Why don't you fuck off, Mister?"

I just stood there, not knowing what to do, unnerved and confused by the sudden obscene expression of his anger, yet feeling somehow guilty and deserving of it.

"Just fuck off, you phony. What have you ever done for Ireland?" He was almost shouting and the people at the bar had

53

stopped talking and they were all looking at us. I admitted quietly that I had done nothing.

"Well don't meddle around with people who are doing something. Fuck off. You hear me?"

I told him I was sorry and backed away and walked over to the end of the bar and stood there, trying to appear casual, as if the fault were Barton's and not mine; as if I were decently avoiding any further provocation that would embarrass others. He was glaring at me as I stood there at the end of the bar and I hoped that my withdrawal would be enough to satisfy him. I resented his intimidation of me but I was frightened by his anger and I knew I had to keep the confrontation simple and clearly and decisively in his favor. He turned from me as suddenly as he had appeared and strode up the bar and out the door, guiding the girl along in front of him.

The beefy blond man came over to me and asked roughly for my identification. I protested my innocence, admitted again that I had done nothing for Ireland, and showed him my driver's license and a business card. He stared at them in the semi-darkness of the bar as if they would reveal some useful truth about me and then handed them back officiously.

"We're a secret military organization, you know. We don't like strangers coming around asking questions about us."

Because the upset had involved the guest of honor, a group of the curious was gathered around us now. Someone asked if I was FBI or CIA. Houlihan was there, and though he knew me only casually, he was responsible for me and I asked him to tell the others I was all right, apologizing again, only too willing to admit to them all that I was nothing but an observer, a person of small consequence, belittling myself so they would not be angry with me.

The group began to break up, realizing nothing important had happened, that it had merely been some misunderstanding, an argument over nothing. I shook hands with the blond man who had questioned me and bought him a glass of beer. The woman who had sung the old rebel songs was sympathetic and told me she thought Barton was drunk and that anyway the bombings were beginning to bother her, if the truth be told. Shooting at soldiers was one thing, she said, and at least it seemed fair, but the bombings were something else again. The blond man, who by then had confided to me that he was a Falls Road boy himself and that there were a lot of British soldiers who would like to know where he was that night, said she didn't understand guerrilla tactics and that, for Christ's sake, how else were you to keep the people out of Belfast and paralyze the city. Didn't she know Nixon was killing thousands of civilians in Vietnam every week?

More people were leaving and the balding schoolteacher took me aside and said he was sure it was the girl who started it. "He thought you were after the girl. You should have popped him one."

"You've got to be kidding," I told him. "An IRA Provisional and I'm going to hit him?" I didn't tell him I hadn't hit anyone in a fight since I was in grade school.

"Why not? You're bigger than he is."

I just gave him one of those looks and a shake of the head. It was over now but all the delicate balance of my worth had been upset by the confrontation. It had not really been a question of standing up to him because the challenge had been only indirectly aimed at my courage. That wasn't the issue. It was my worth.

The leader of the trio announced the party was over. He thanked everybody for being such a good audience and then they played "God Bless America" and he sang it while two men stood beside him with an American flag stretched out between them. Some of the people at the tables stood at the start of the song, remembering Kate Smith and the war, or mistaking it for the national anthem, but then when the flag was unfurled, everybody stood except those who were too drunk or who were arguing at the tables in the back.

When I left I walked to my car in the middle of the street for those few familiar New York City blocks, looking to either side of me and behind, feeling foolish but thinking of the suspected spies and informers found in Belfast alleys with hoods over their heads, a bullet through their brains, and of others shot through the knees, so that for the rest of their crippled lives they would remember the IRA. Hadn't the old carpenter from Mayo made a point of telling me they had no conscience?

I brooded on Eddie Barton all the way home. He was a wanted man, a criminal to some, maybe, but a man of action, and I was not. His rejection of me was a dismissal of my person as irrelevant. It was impossible to think of ever communicating anything about myself to somebody like him. There were no shared grounds of judgment between us where one could slip and slide, tell funny stories, account for failures or modestly put forward accomplishments for consideration; in short, be nice to know. Not with a man who was capable of killing you.

The Sunday night traffic on the East River Drive was light and driving along with the tall New York apartment houses on my left, I imagined myself back in Belfast, in the Lower Falls or the Ardoyne, or wherever it was the Provisional headquarters were, delivering a pistol that I would have smuggled into Ireland, dismantled in a plaster cast on my leg, or counting out a thousand dollars on an oilcloth-topped table in a ghetto kitchen, money that I would personally raise through my talents and ingenuity, and I would say, "Eddie Barton, here is something I have done for Ireland."

PART II

one

Father Riordan was one of those who didn't think much of the Irish. They were good for a laugh, maybe, but impractical and too sentimental for his tastes; too much given to the booze and a song or a wild dream.

Father Riordan was an old-style Jesuit and despite his name, English, not Irish. In that two- or three-year period when he came over to America summers, we would meet occasionally for drinks and a steak and sometimes sit talking at the table until the restaurant closed. He was in his middle fifties then, with a strong, ruddy face and straight steel gray hair. There was a good-natured self-assurance about him that I found pleasing and appropriately paternal. He was worldly wise in that Jesuit way; not one to be deferential, except sometimes to be polite or to keep a conversation going, but nice about it because he was enthusiastic and interested in what we talked about. He was a proud man yet open about it. I didn't know him well enough to know his failings, but because he was a priest, I'd have said that pride must have been the sin he never mastered.

Some of the things he felt superior about were things that my background had taught me to admire. Being a Jesuit, of course, mattered to him a great deal, but being English and Catholic mattered too. The name of Riordan was accidental. It came from some male ancestor who had left Ireland and settled in London, but that was a long time ago and hardly any fault of his. Except for that one Irishman, his forebears had all been men and women of breeding whose Catholic lives were intertwined with English history. They were not ignorant Paddys in a bog somewhere with no knowledge of doctrine and no choice to be other than they were. His people had kept the Faith through Tudor times and under Stuart kings and during Cromwell. When Catholics throughout England were being persecuted, or were leaving the Church to find some new concept of Christianity more to their liking, or betraying it to keep their heads, his people were among those who had remained loyal.

The idea of the Church martyred through all those years of English history, that I knew only piecemeal and through scenes remembered out of context from books and plays and movies, was part of my Catholic heritage, too, and far more meaningful to me in terms of religious melodrama than any story of early Christians thrown to the lions or of missionaries murdered by natives for preaching a strange faith in an alien land. The past that he valued, English-speaking and recognizable, was an outsider's past and it had little to do with dutiful passivity or the parish dances and Monday night novenas of the Catholic establishment world I had been raised in.

Father Riordan taught moral theology to candidate Jesuits somewhere back in England, but in those years he used to come over during the summer on a teaching exchange program with a Jesuit college outside New York. When the summer sessions were finished he would stay a few weeks longer at our parish, where he had friends, filling in for one of the secular priests on vacation and impressing the parishioners with his witty observations from the pulpit at Sunday Mass. Usually there are no sermons during the summer in Catholic churches, but he would say a few words at least because he was good at it and confident that hearing him would be worth the extra five minutes, even on a humid end-of-August Sunday.

He had known Evelyn Waugh and once we talked about *Brideshead Revisited* while a restaurant emptied and two waitresses sat and drank coffee at another table, and I was surprised at the pleasure it gave me then and afterward that a book I'd not read in a dozen years should have contained so rich a lode as to justify more than an hour's conversation. That was the night I said something about Irish Catholicism being a special kind of religious experience, assuming he was Irish, despite his accent, because of his name, and he had dismissed the Irish as a superstitious lot and not to be taken seriously and talked instead about the Church in England.

Graham Greene, too, was an acquaintance of his, but in Father Riordan's eyes too much the self-indulgent boy still, with his wandering around the world looking for excitement to relieve his boredom and his bleak, haunted, half-held faith. There was usually some point of fact or feeling behind Father Riordan's opinions that was different from what others I knew might have said, and stimulating though our discussions were, they were always weighted in his favor. Nevertheless, I preferred Greene to Waugh and I would have liked it if he had known him better. It was a fan's reaction, as if his knowing someone of prominence would make him like that person too.

Because he was from England and a Jesuit and talked so well, he was much in demand with couples who wanted to show him off to their non-Catholic friends over cocktails or at dinner parties. His looks and manner made him a favorite of women, especially those approaching middle age who had once been English majors but who were now always tan from tennis and who drank too much. At those parties there was always the chance that someone, perhaps one of the tan-legged women, or a husband who also drank too much, and who disliked the way his life had turned out, would be overcome by gin and the presence of a worldly Jesuit and try to corner him alone to confess some impossible romance or to tell him painfully and in slurred words that they no longer believed. That still happened in Catholic circles then. It went with the Roman collar and being a priest who liked to socialize.

Father Riordan liked these people, liked being important to them, I'm sure, and even enjoyed being displayed at their parties. He was sorry for the lives they could not change and if he was cornered with the admission of some private guilt, he'd pass no judgment but just say something about God not only being a father, whose love had to be earned, but a mother as well, who loved whether it was deserved or not and who would pick you up again like a child no matter how many times you stumbled.

But I was a man who didn't want to be helped, who was past asking for clarification of his doubts or confessing any more to sin. Those few dinners, talking about books and history and social change, about ideas of God and authority, were enough for me. The talking was my confession, and I'm sure he knew it.

Liking conversation as he did, he was puzzled by American drinking habits as he had observed them at the various parties he'd attended, where half the guests would be stupefied with martinis by the time the meal was served. He saw the ideal evening as perhaps one whiskey and then the meal, a hearty one with some good wine to highlight it, and maybe a brandy afterward with coffee. Then if you wanted to drink and talk, argue some fine point of moral theology or Church doctrine, put a bottle of scotch on the table and go at it until three in the morning if you liked, but on a full stomach.

That was the way he would sometimes drink when the old Jesuits he'd been ordained with gathered at the provincial house back in England. It would be a homecoming of "Js", as he called them, who had been posted to institutions of learning all over the world, and when they got together at dinner, talking over the roast and the wine and the brandy, the impression he gave was that the level of discourse would be such as to astound the twenty-eight- and thirty-year-old seminarians who stood around like children at a parents' party.

There was something almost outrageously arrogant about that story and I liked it, particularly the idea that men near thirty should be pictured as standing almost slack-jawed in wonder in the presence of their elders and betters, still not qualified to do more than listen or ask an occasional question. Except for Father Riordan, I only knew the Jesuits by reputation. To Catholics of my time, they were supposed to be the best, the elite guard of the Church. I had accepted that about them and there was a mystique about the word *Jesuit* for me, but still I was surprised to hear him speak so boastfully.

Late one night several years after I'd last seen Father Riordan, after I heard he'd had a nervous breakdown and was hospitalized back in England, a man, after all, as fragile as any other, I was standing in a bar outside Boston with some friends drinking beer and eating peanuts. Everyone was young and Janis Joplin was singing "Me and Bobby Magee" on the jukebox so loud it was hard to hear anything else. There was a big barrel of peanuts by the wall across from the bar and on the wall there were notices advertising apartments for rent and offering motorcycles and cars and guitars for sale, and above the barrel there was a cartoon drawing of Mr. Natural, the dirty old man of the counter-culture comic books, illustrating some announcement that was headlined "Quest Into the Unknown." Next to it there was a color poster of two bugs that appeared to be copulating on a leaf of grass.

I stood breaking open the peanuts and eating them and looked at the poster. I knew that it probably was meant to say that all the world was Love, or at least should be making love, but I saw it as cheap and gross and the meaningless flicker of bug lust on the green leaf depressed me, along with the thought of the seedy, all-purpose novelty store that it came from. I squinted at it and the cartoon of the dirty old man, to see them differently if I could, the way an artist would with a painting, and then said to hell with it and went back to the bar with the inane thought that a Jesuit could handle it.

I don't know why I thought that. It was not one of my nights for pontificating on religion and certainly I had known things that were far more depressing and meaningless than that picture of the copulating bugs. I didn't need the Jesuits to explain that to me. But it was late and there was the taste of too many cigarettes and too many beers in my mouth and perhaps I felt out of place with the touchstones of people who were all younger than I was.

With the noise from the jukebox as loud as it was it would have taken more effort than I wanted to give to have heard and understood what my friends at the bar were talking about, so I pretended I was listening and created a scene in my mind from Father Riordan's story about the old "Js" returned to England from around the world. I made it a rainy evening and they were gathered before dinner in some large, high-ceilinged library, all wood-paneled with heavy gilt-framed paintings of scholarly priests long dead, and large, leaded glass windows, and a huge fireplace with a fire burning. There in that library in my mind were men who stood among the great intellects of the world, schooled in argument to defend the Faith, and who each day, too, spoke the words *Hoc est corpus meum* to consecrate the Host and magically recreate the presence of Christ. There, all in black, with that rectangular spot of white at the throat, was the collective totality of the world and the spirit embodied for the Church in the Society of Jesus, as if all knowledge flowed through them and could be accounted for in their argumentation and discourse, *ad majorem Dei gloriam.*

I still wonder at how it all came to mean so much to me. I was only occasionally religious, was almost always inattentive at Mass, knew only odds and ends of dogma and theology. Why is it that I regard my Catholic past as if I am a survivor of some extraordinary experience; as if I had come down with the Marines from the Chosin Reservoir or had been with the 101st Airborne at Bastogne?

All that time when I was little my faith was a subject taught by nuns at Sunday school and I learned it in the same way that I learned arithmetic or geography, except that the truths of the catechism dealt with definitions and concepts that were to be far more consequential in their implications for my person. It was not the same at all as merely believing in God or that one should be good rather than bad, yet through those years the Church was just there. I didn't analyze it or question it; I hardly thought about it. Certainly I didn't consider it in any such grandiose terms as constituting the grounds of my being, but that's what it turns out to have been, because even at seven and nine years old, everything that I was learning, the arithmetic and the geography, and everything else that I was, was secondary to the fact that I was Catholic. That was the final and ultimate thing that could be said about me.

Losing such a sense of self as that is painful and can take a long time. Some people never get over it and I am clearly one of them. When it happened to me it was like a man falling overboard in the middle of the ocean and seeing the ship grow smaller in the distance and then realizing there is nothing but the gray water and the gray sky and himself alone in the ocean swells. Not that I felt that way all the time, because I didn't, but the feeling of loss, of having been abandoned, was always in the background.

That was in college and the Army, the time-honored period of religious crisis in a young man's life, when I was still hoping there would be a way to proceed from Catholicism to another view of myself that provided absolutes which would be as comforting.

Long before the questions of worth and purpose were equated with the humbling experience of Confession, before the forming of a psychological dependency on the pendulum swings of anx-

65

iety and guilt, and then relief through the cleansing humiliation of admission of sin, forehead pressed against the screen that separates one from the priest in a dark confessional box, there was a small altar in the corner of my room and on it a rough, handmade stone grotto of Our Lady of Lourdes that the doorman in the apartment house where I lived built from a large-sized pineapple juice can.

That was a hobby of his, making those replicas of the grotto at Lourdes. He and his wife were both small, slight, gray-haired people who to me seemed old but who were probably then only in their early fifties. They were a quiet, childless couple. The wife did sewing for women in the apartment house and he made grottos out of pineapple cans.

I watched him make the one he did for me. It was his day off and I sat on the linoleum-covered floor of the little living room in his basement apartment and a baseball game was on the radio and Joe Dimaggio was the star. It took almost all of the afternoon for him to cut away one side of the can and glue small stones to the tin inside and out so that it would have a cave-like look, and when it was finished he glued a cheap plaster statue of Our Lady to the stone base he had built up on the bottom.

I was eight then, maybe the beginning of nine, and I used to say my prayers at that little altar with the grotto on it, and there was a small candle that I would light in front of it, one of those short, thick religious candles in a round jar-like container that probably served as a night light as well and made me feel that I was being watched over by the Blessed Mother.

The altar and the grotto were gone by the time I was ten, of that I'm sure, because I moved to the back room early that year and the altar was never part of it. Perhaps I rebelled at so much holiness. More likely the necessity of a desk on which to do schoolwork was considered a more important piece of furniture than an altar for a boy in the fourth grade. I do know that the radio broadcast of that baseball game, though incidental, has always been part of my memory of the grotto, as if the young

66

Dimaggio's hitting a home run, or whatever it was he did to be identified with the day it was made, provided an unconscious protective association, a masculine balance that I must always have felt was required.

The doorman's job was done away with about the same time as my altar; at least there never was another doorman after he left. Whether his falling down and breaking his glasses and cutting his face on another day off had anything to do with his leaving, I never knew. I was playing with some boys in a field and I saw him stumble and fall coming down the hill from where the stores were. We ran over to where he was struggling to sit up, and even though I had the sense that he wasn't badly hurt, it upset me to see him stunned and confused, with blood on his face. Some men came and took him up the block to the apartment house in a car and we were told he had simply tripped, as anyone could, but I knew he was drunk and that bothered me.

One night a few years ago, after coming home late from a party, I sat alone in the living room of my home with a glass of milk and some cake and read through my high school yearbook. I had found it in the cellar earlier that week and brought it upstairs to look at when I had the time. My wife said she was exhausted and went directly to bed but I sat there and read all the inscriptions and messages that had been written in it during those last days of high school, paying particular attention to the ones from girls I had liked or who I knew had liked me, and some of them were flattering and made me feel quite the fellow sitting there reading them again at two o'clock in the morning after almost twenty-five years.

There were inscriptions throughout the book, many of them signed with fraternity and sorority symbols and first names that no longer went with any face and they referred to games played and races run, to meetings and conversations I could no longer remember. Then I read a message from a red-headed girl with an Irish name who was a friend of some of the girls I took out

67

then, and she had written that parties were never dull when I was there, and I enjoyed reading that about myself and I remembered how I would recite Kipling's poems and do vaudeville routines with Speedy Thomas.

I turned the book around to read the postscript she had written vertically in the margin next to her picture—"I still say you should be a priest"—and I started to cry. I don't know that there were any grounds for those words; it had probably been a kind of joke between us and not meant to be serious, because in those days the idea of a priest that most of us would have had was Bing Crosby singing at a piano in a baseball cap. But it was unexpectedly serious to me alone in the living room at two in the morning twenty-three years later to think that I might have impressed this girl as something other than a party bright boy reciting "Gunga Din."

I never was even an altar boy, yet it is one of the peculiarities of my disbelief that I still accept that the office of priesthood exceeds individuality; that good or bad, present or absent, once a priest always a priest.

There are undoubtedly men who are selling shoes today, or in advertising, or teaching school, who were priests once and who would dismiss my views on Holy Orders as typical of someone who likes to sentimentalize about his Catholic past and who doesn't know what it is to be a priest. So be it. I idealize the priesthood. I know it is made up of ordinary men like myself and that their reasons for becoming priests were not necessarily profound and that they sometimes come to see their lives differently and change their minds about what they're doing and decide to be something else. And if it causes them trouble to do that, they can see a psychiatrist and perhaps work out their childhood conflicts and their guilts and then function better in their new role of not being priests any more.

I know, too, that most of the world's population is completely indifferent to the Catholic Church and that hundreds of millions

68

of people probably care deeply about things that would never have any meaning to me, and that in this light, the importance of the Roman Catholic priesthood in my own background and culture is clearly accidental and nothing more. But those facts don't really have anything to do with what I feel. I am impressed still with the idea that a man could think there is such a thing as an irrevocable commitment to the Church that will change his life—change his person, even—that once made cannot be unmade, because it is beyond reason and therefore of a different dimension from taking a job or choosing a career.

Being a social worker or a good guy supervising the parish basketball program are fine and worthwhile things to do, but you don't have to be a priest to do them. You can work for the Peace Corps or the YMCA and be involved in Christian action. What makes a priest different is not that he should instruct the ignorant, aid the poor, or comfort the sick and the dying, or even that he renounce the world and its pleasures, family, and fortune, to dedicate himself to those ends. In many instances he may be too inept a man, too selfish, too vain, to do those things well, and he is less a priest because of it, but a priest nonetheless.

What makes a priest different from other men, including those who are better men than he, is that of the powers attributed to him there is one that is awesome. He can change the basic reality of bread and wine into the body and blood of Christ. The bread and wine don't *represent* the body and blood of Christ; they're not props in a shared communal experience acknowledging dependence on a supreme being for our spiritual and material sustenance. That's sensible Protestant thinking. When a priest consecrates the bread and wine it actually *becomes* Christ, and that's an outrageous claim. That's magic. It is beyond all reason to believe that, yet I am intimidated still by the fact that I believed it once.

By the time I married, and with children and respectability, it began to seem as if losing my faith wasn't all that important. I acted out being Catholic again, saying it was for my Catholic wife and in-laws and for my mother, and in time I became more devout in that pretense than I ever had been when I believed. After all, I said to myself, Catholicism was my heritage and I was psychologically comfortable with its forms. It offered a rich and interesting way to interpret experience and a man who observed its disciplines, confessed his sins and received Communion regularly, thought much about his faults and imperfections and wanted to be better, had to derive some useful benefits from the practice of it. It all seemed very reasonable and responsible.

Somewhere, maybe from Aquinas, I had acquired the idea that there was no situation in life that was not a moral one and a friend of mine at work named Eamon Brennan used to kid me about that and call me a virtue seeker. He was my religious friend, yet we only talked about religion sometimes. Mostly it was about our jobs and our chances of getting another fifteen dollars a week; about Ireland, because his father and mother had been born there; and about the pretty receptionists and stenographers we might have dated if we weren't young married fathers of families.

Eamon had been a scholarship student all through school with the Jesuits and had studied two years to be one himself before he realized he didn't have a vocation and left the seminary. By the time I knew him he had four children, and because the children had all been born one after another, he had come to reject the Church's position on birth control. This was before Catholics tended to go their own way without guilt in this matter and for someone like Eamon, raised in the rigidities of Jesuit thinking, it was impossible to hold for long that the Church was wrong on this one issue and right in everything else. He had no choice but to accept the sinfulness of contraception or get out, because if the Church wasn't right, wasn't all he had believed it to be, then it was like any other church, decent and Christian and nothing more, and his being Catholic or not didn't matter. Eamon was one of those who had to have everything, and believing, I think, far more than I, he left.

There was an early April evening from that time that is clear to me still and that defines the way we were. It was during Eamon's last months of deliberation over whether or not to leave the Church and we were walking up Park Avenue with Joe Daly, one of his friends from the public relations firm where he worked. We were on our way to a cocktail party at the Waldorf that was being given to promote a new line of asphalt shingles to the trade magazines and newspapers. The shingle manufacturer was a client of their firm and they were going to the party to help fill it out so it would have the appearance of success and I was going along with them because I was their friend and to help fill it out more.

There was still that sense of sun behind the buildings and the evening was just beginning to turn gray and the new spring was in it and all things seemed possible. We were striding purposefully along to the party and Joe commented exuberantly about our being three young Irishmen on the make. It was an open remark that could have meant anything and it had more to do with the excitement that was in the evening than anything else.

I remember feeling pleased that I was included because those were the years when I was coming more and more to see myself as Irish, drawing on my distant family past, and the two of them were clearly more Irish than I. The light was against us at Forty-seventh Street and we stood at the corner and one of those old Hasidic Jews in a long black coat to his ankles and a broad-brimmed black hat and a tieless white shirt buttoned at the collar was standing beside us. After the light changed and we'd crossed and were walking ahead, Eamon asked if we'd seen the crazy-looking old guy with the wispy beard and the curls hanging down around his ears who was shambling along behind us. "Mind you, I'm not against the Jews of any variety, because some

71

of my best friends are chosen people, including the ones who pay my salary every week, but I ask you, didn't he look crazy? Didn't he look as if he should be put away?"

Joe and I agreed that the old man looked crazy but Joe said that the Constitution guaranteed him that right. Eamon said that wasn't the point. The point was that anybody who'd take the trouble to be honest about it would say the old Jew looked crazy and he looked that way because he and all the others like him that you see on the streets of New York believed in things that had nothing to do with the reality of living in the world.

"But he thinks he's right," I said. "He thinks it's us who are crazy walking along with our briefcases. We're the crazy ones to him."

"So what are you getting at," Joe asked. "That we're crazy? We already know that."

"No we don't," Eamon said. "We don't think we're just as irrational in what we believe as he is. The only difference is with us it doesn't show. It's all inside our heads. Maybe we don't put our hair in curlers and go tripping around over our coats, but are you going to tell me it's saner to believe that God became Man just one time and was crucified to redeem our sins and then rose again from the dead and went to Heaven and left us the Pope and Holy Mother Church to get us to Heaven, too, so we could join Him there? And that every day, all over the world, Christ comes back to us in the form of a wafer so we can eat Him and the only place you'll find Him is hidden away in the tabernacle of a Catholic church? You don't think that's crazy?"

Joe and I agreed that it was and we added other outrageous things that Catholics believe and we were very glib because the three of us were clever with words and it was important when we were together to be fast and amusing, whatever we talked about, and we laughed at our remarks and the madness of being Catholic and were still making observations about the faith that none of us would probably ever get over as we went up on the elevator at the Waldorf to the suite where the cocktail party was being held.

Some months after that, maybe six months, maybe a year, Eamon and I got our better jobs, and then better jobs after those, and we lost track of one another and I don't know how he handled not being Catholic any more or how he is today. My own accomodation was largely based on guilt and I stayed on. It was because of a priest, as much as anything else, that I finally left. He was younger than I and I knew him only on the altar and to nod to if I saw him on the street, but I liked him for going against the grain with sermons that were relevant to current social issues before that sort of talk from the pulpit became common in suburban parishes. Sometimes he would speak about the early days of the Church when Christianity was still a Jewish movement, and I liked that, too, because most of the Catholics I knew didn't want to think of their religion that way; didn't want to be jammed by any historical truth about its origins that challenged their comfortable superiority in a society that still subtly discriminated against the Jews, and knowing that, I felt superior.

One February Sunday, irritated by the fact that so many of the faces in front of him were bored and inattentive, were staring up at the windows, he said that a person should not bother coming to Mass if it was just a matter of habit. If a man or a woman didn't believe in the presence of God on that altar, then be honest enough to stay home, because the day he, Father Shea, stopped believing would be the last day they'd see him there.

Those words challenged me. They made not believing as serious a matter as believing, and I took them seriously and left before the Mass was finished.

two

Jack Donovan was my Irish cultural friend. I didn't really like him when I first met him and there was no reason at all to think we'd become good friends or to suspect that he was the kind of person who played the bagpipes in an Irish pipe band as a hobby.

Maybe it was that he was so big, like a basketball player almost, though filled out with middle age, and it had made him self-conscious so that he always needed to assert himself as capable and prove that he had a head on his shoulders and was not just physically intimidating.

The way I met him had a lot to do with it, of course. It was at a three-day economic seminar for corporate executives at the Council on Foreign Relations. I worked there then and one of the things I did was act as host at the seminars. The Council had about it the imposing aura of a first-rate gentleman's club and a reputation as a foreign policy think tank, and the seminars were occasions where everyone presented an efficiently respectable face. Though I did this too, I was inclined to suspect that it came more naturally to most of the men who attended than it did to me.

Jack Donovan was an executive with an investment firm, a pleasant man whenever we talked during the coffee breaks or over cocktails before the lunches or dinners, but the impression he gave was that business was the important thing, that the way he earned his money counted for more than anything else. I would never have known that there was more to him than investments, that he was in love with the idea of Ireland and had loved, too, the sound of bagpipes since he was a boy, if I hadn't told him the story of the rag-tag Irish group that had demonstrated outside the Council the night of the dinner for Prime Minister Wilson.

This was before the riots and the bombings in Northern Ireland and the murders on the back streets of the Belfast ghettos, and a half dozen years after the IRA's long campaign against the border had fizzled out in 1962. The affair was a hastily arranged one and somehow a small band of die-hard Republican sympathizers from the Bronx or Queens got word of it. It was late in a winter afternoon when they arrived and at first there were only six or eight of them. They made their signs in front of the Council with crayons and the kind of white poster paper you buy at the neighborhood stationer's, using the hood of a parked car or the pavement to write against. GET BRITISH TROOPS OUT OF IRELAND. GIVE US BACK THE SIX COUNTIES. BRITAIN GO HOME.

Inside, the few staff members who noticed were laughing because the men parading in a circle on the street in front of the building seemed the knockabout kind you could picture wasting away afternoons over shots of rye and beer in an Irish bar underneath an El somewhere, and here they were outside the Council on Foreign Relations on upper Park Avenue. Their sullen seriousness seemed ridiculous, even to me, who enjoyed singing songs and talking about the old days of rebellion with flying columns of the IRA coming down from the hills and Michael Collins riding unconcerned through the streets of Dublin on a bicycle with a price of ten thousand pounds on his head. That was for fun, like being a Civil War buff or a collector of baseball cards. The facts were that Northern Ireland was part of Great Britain and had been for almost fifty years. Everyone knew that.

75

Even the Catholics there had been indifferent to the IRA's last attempt to fight partition, a laboriously planned campaign that ended in death or long imprisonment for many of those who took part in it, and it was a joke. Yet men like these pickets, with nothing better to do, refused to recognize that and nurtured old dreams and angers that were no longer relevant.

I was the Council's resident Irishman, self-appointed, and in that role, I claimed the men on the street as my own and I said that I was going out as an emissary to make sure they didn't throw bricks through the windows. Outside, cold in just a suit and vest, I kidded with the group in windbreakers and work coats, pretending that I was like them, and I told them to remember there was an Irishman on the premises whose family came from Dublin. A fat man with several front teeth missing asked me what I was doing toadying to the likes of Wilson if I was Irish, and I told him I only worked there and couldn't approve the dinner guests and that Wilson didn't even know that I existed.

Back inside again, there was some joking about my negotiating with a foreign adversary. Someone said I should get thirty dollars from petty cash and take the whole bunch of them to Third Avenue for drinks and that would solve the problem. I went along with all of it because I shared the comfortable superiority of being with the Council and I was quite willing to have these working-class Irishmen dismissed as drunks and I, too, thought it was amusing to see them milling around in a circle in front of our door with schoolboy signs you could hardly read proclaiming a cause that was long dead. GIVE US BACK THE SIX COUNTIES, for Christ's sake. They're gone! Those are Scots Presbyterians there now, and for more than three hundred years. Forget the Six Counties. The Protestants own them.

I went about my business and then it was dark and drawing close to the time when Wilson was due to arrive and the group outside was up to over a dozen with those who had come over after work. One of them put a Clancy Brothers album of rebel songs on a battery-run record player and they started to chant,

"Britain out of Ireland." After all the waiting, it was a sudden thing when the two big black limousines of Wilson's party arrived at the curb. The windbreakered men were shouting and crowding around the cars and a half dozen policemen were in the middle of them, shoving them back, and Wilson was out on the sidewalk surrounded by aides and through the door and into the Council in a matter of seconds.

There weren't any big purposeful Irish–American picket lines then and once Wilson was inside, it was over and there was nothing more for them to do but go home. But they had waited for so long to shout their anger for those few seconds that some of them kept shouting still at our windows and at the empty street and the buildings around us, and two of them unfurled a British flag and tried to set it on fire. It wouldn't ignite at first and by the time it did, several of the policemen who had stood by good-naturedly during the picketing, and who had forced themselves for the sake of order between Wilson and the windbreakered men, saw what was happening and intervened. Only a few inches were burned from the corner before the fire was stamped out and the flag taken away.

I watched all this from a third-floor window and I remember wishing that I had that flag, thinking that its charred corner would mean something to me, that it expressed an ill-defined resentment of my own. But instead of going out to the police and asking for it, bluffing them with my Council connection, I went down to the cocktail reception for Wilson, where all the men were well-bred and successful in dark business suits, and where I was jokingly introduced to one of the Prime Minister's aides as the culprit responsible for the disturbance out on the street. I pretended to be embarrassed and denied any association with the kind of men who had tried to burn the British flag. It was all very light and witty and I finished my drink and left the reception and went to a bar, more sad than not because the Irish were such clowns.

Telling the story to three or four executives over coffee during a morning break at the seminar almost a year and a half later, I didn't tell it that way. I meant it only as an illustration of the occasional minor harrassments that were directed at the Council, the little excitements of life on Sixty-Eighth Street and Park Avenue, and I made it funny. The reference to my own Irish sympathies was a lighthearted one, but afterwards, when we were going back into the meeting on foreign trade with Rumania, Donovan put a hand on my shoulder and suggested we have lunch and talk some more about the Irish once the seminar was over.

Jack Donovan once spoke to a small meeting of visiting representatives of the Irish Government about investments or finance, and he told me he started with the remark, "I am the only man here not born in his native land." It was meant for a laugh, or at least to make everyone feel comfortable with the idea that here was an American who was sympathetic to Irish problems, but that was really the way Donovan had come to feel; that was the way he wanted to see himself in relation to Ireland. I don't know why it was like that for him. He was from Iowa, which is not a state I associated with Irish settlement, Anglo-Irish as I was and at least as far removed in time from Ireland.

At our first lunch the week following the seminar I told him that my connections with Ireland were actually somewhat tenuous and based on two great-grandfathers and a great-grandmother I knew nothing about. I was self-conscious about making too much of it and quite willing to dismiss it as an enthusiasm to which I was not truly entitled, but Donovan would have none of that. "My connections are just as remote as yours if we're going to judge by time," he told me, "but they are anything but tenuous."

This was in the spring of 1969, three months before the riots that burned out almost two hundred homes in the Catholic ghetto districts of the Falls Road and the Ardoyne in Belfast. There was no internment camp at Long Kesh. Bloody Sunday hadn't hap-

78

pened yet in Derry. This was before the nightly newscasts reported the day's violence in the North and changed the placid image of Ireland promoted on radio commercials by the lilting brogues of *Aer Lingus* stewardesses and made it a country to be puzzled about, despaired over, taken seriously. You didn't often meet people like Donovan then.

I could understand someone caring about nationality, be it Irish or whatever, but not the way Donovan did when he was three generations removed and raised in the state of Iowa. I was too much aware that I had in a sense created myself as Irish to speak of Ireland the way he did. I was as entitled to be Irish as he was, but it still seemed an acquired thing to me.

It is difficult now to remember just how it started with me but I think it was a reaction to work and the respectability of fathering a family. Not work in the sense of earning one's way in life, but the fact that I had accepted the confinements of an office routine in a job I didn't like, felt guilty about being five minutes late in the morning or coming back from lunch, suited up with shined shoes every day and one winter wore a felt hat as a badge of new maturity. That was a dozen years and more before I met Donovan, long before I qualified to take a whiskey in the presence of a Prime Minister. I knew little about Ireland then but I had the romantic idea that by declaring myself an Irishman I was somehow asserting myself against the fact that I was doing well in a meaningless position; that there was a part of me that was a rebel, a free spirit and Celtic dreamer and beyond the limitations of being a young man on the rise with a new briefcase filled with office papers—as if there weren't Irish working all over New York, assiduously seeking advancement, buying insurance, riding commuter trains, and raising families in the suburbs.

It was not something I thought that much about, but it was the beginning. I toyed with it from time to time, trotted it out to sing songs with at parties, used it to kid with secretaries and impress them, played with it for fun, laying on a brogue talking with the Irish woman who had helped to raise my wife and who came out of sentiment for those days to help her with our own children when they were young. It was an easy matter. I bore no ethnic burden. Eamon Brennan, the religious friend of my late twenties, the ambitious publicist whose departure from the Church was such an occasion of crisis, told me that I wouldn't think it was such a great thing if I'd been shit-faced shanty Irish as he had, growing up and running errands after school for his father's corner grocery store in Brooklyn. He was probably right. There was no poverty identified with race in my background; no humble, balding parent with the mark of the foreign born in his speech to be ashamed of. My resentments were less precise.

To me, then, it was a way of presenting myself as different. With a name that blandly conveyed the real America, I could have been Anglo-Saxon if I wanted to. I could claim the soldiers and officers of my father's Confederate family, the surgeon who amputated four legs at the Battle of the Wilderness, the minister who in 1826 founded the Baptist Church in Clarksville, Tennessee, the distant aunt who was a niece of Thomas Jefferson. I could trace my lineage back to pre-Revolutionary War times in the Virginia Colony. I could imagine ties to the courts of English kings. And I did think that way about myself sometimes. There was a period after college when I referred to some of that past occasionally, traded on it in conversations where such references came up naturally, amusingly, *pointedly,* perhaps at some party with young men in gray flannel and tattersall vests and black knit ties and girls who had come out at debutante balls. I knew such things were of little consequence. I used to make fun of those references to distinguished antecedents that appeared in announcements of weddings and engagements in the local newspaper. Still, those were the claims that went with belonging, and they were associated with well-bred Protestants who had money and status, and for a time I wanted to be like them and to have them see me that way, too. I had the right. My credentials were

legitimate. But something in me finally made me say to hell with the Protestant Yalies and instead, for reasons obvious to me now —reasons that were embarrassingly superficial and adolescent, and other reasons that were far more complicated, that cannot be easily understood, because they expressed something of a Catholic's mind and sense of person, an outsider's pride and resentment—I chose to be Irish.

What it was that made Donovan care so much about Ireland, I never knew. By the time I met him, the commitment was a *given,* take it or leave it. He was not inclined to analyze it, at least not for me. It was like asking a priest why he was a priest. There was this and there was that and there was the other, and beyond that there was nothing you could say. When he first told me about claiming Ireland as his native land, it seemed to me presumptuous and I was surprised and amused that this big, graying executive from an investment firm, who had seemed so ordinarily able and efficient, would talk that way. I should have been able to appreciate by then that a native land can exist in the mind, be an idea, a fantasy, but I didn't. That still seemed a foolish thing to me. I could understand wishing for something other than what you had; to long for a life on the Greek Islands, say, or in Arizona or the Great Northwest, but that was different. Donovan didn't want a way of life so much as a past that was more than Correctionville, Iowa. He wanted roots that went deeper, something that would provide the accident of his present with greater meaning. What he was talking about was what I, too, wanted, but didn't fully realize yet: a definition of self that had a richer texture to it than could be derived just from the years you had lived, or from a career and a club membership, a mortgaged home and a wife and children. It was a yearning for tribal identity.

My story of the shabby Irish protest group demonstrating outside the Council didn't mean anything to Donovan except that it revealed something about me. It showed I was interested in Ireland and therefore a potential friend from a work milieu that did

81

not contain too many men who were. Though he claimed a forebear who had been executed in Wexford after the Rebellion of 1798, which gave his past a more militant turn than mine, to my knowledge, possessed, modern Republicanism mattered not at all to him. He was glad enough, I'm sure, that there had been an Easter Rising and that the Twenty-Six Counties, at least, had achieved their independence, but even that amused him. "Do you know how many old men there are walking around today who claim they were in the Post Office during Easter Week?" he asked me once. "Thousands. They would have had to stack them in layers to fit in all the old bar flies who say they were there."

Later, when we knew each other better, he used to kid me about my Council story. "Leave it to you to get sentimental about a bunch of bums wandering around in the dark shouting about the border." To him the border was there and that was that. What happened in the North didn't concern him. People up there were different. They didn't want to be Irish to begin with. As for the IRA, it was a fine organization if you liked gunmen and psychotic troublemakers, men who were against everything his upbringing stood for and all he had accomplished with his life. If you wanted to talk about rebels, give him the men of '98. Not the rabble in the countryside, the peasants with their pikes, but the lawyers and intelligent men of means who had conceived the rising and conspired with the French. Give him, even, the old Gaelic chieftains doing battle with Anglo-Norman adventurers, fighting to maintain a culture and a way of life down through the time of Elizabeth. He liked rebellion best when it involved people of high station.

Except for the scenery, the lakes and hills, the quaint small village streets, the great country houses and ruined castles, what he liked about Ireland had almost nothing to do with the present day. It was the music and the poetry and the stories of olden times that he cared about.

So it turned out that Jack Donovan and I had Ireland in common and that was how the friendship started. To me, though, what we shared was not so much Ireland as the fact that we both found the idea of Ireland important. I enjoyed him and I learned a lot from him, because he was well-read in Ireland's history and could cite the legalities used by Henry VIII to acquire the lands of Hugh O'Neill and Hugh O'Donnell, and explain what they came to mean in the subsequent years of Ireland's relations with England, but what I liked most about him was that he cared so much about something that had nothing to do with the way he earned his living, that in certain respects even ran counter to everything the New York work world represented.

Donovan could afford the attitude that a job was what you did to pay your bills because he was very well-to-do, not only from the investment business but from his marriage. Yet for all his talk, he had only been to Ireland once and he knew he was never going to move there because he had two children in private schools and a comfortable way of life that he didn't really want to change. What he wanted was some kind of business arrangement on the side that would permit him to go there on short trips and write off the costs. Once it was almost oysters.

We were sailing on his boat when he first told me about it. It was a summer Sunday and we were tacking somewhere off Greenwich, trying to work our way back to the mooring without having to use the engine, and he told me about a friend of his whose family had inherited a house and shorefront property in County Sligo on Ballysodare Bay. The property included oyster beds along the shore that had once been famous in restaurants throughout Ireland and England but which had been dormant for fifty years and more. Donovan said the Irish Government was very interested in attracting foreign investment and he was full of ideas about how to get investors because his friend had told him there was a lot of money to be made in oysters. What was needed was someone who knew how to farm them and a plan for developing the beds.

83

I had been lying back watching the dozens of small white patches the sails of other boats made all around us in the distance, looking at the water and the late afternoon sky and thinking of the good things I always associated with water and late day in summer, and the idea of oysters on Ballysodare Bay sounded very attractive. We talked about how great it could be back at his house over drinks and dinner and for months afterward we were both excited about the prospect of raising money for a business venture in Ireland. We'd meet at his office after work, sometimes with the friend who had inherited the property, or with oystermen from Long Island and Connecticut, and there was a great deal of correspondence back and forth with the Irish Government. Weekends we'd read over all the data we were collecting on the oyster industry, calculate capital needs, project the growth rate of oysters and their probable market price, and the figures were intoxicating.

The combination of Ireland and Yeats country in Sligo and food from the sea touched our imaginations and our desire to be involved with something more than impersonal business enterprises that might or might not make a profit, and of course our figures were very impressive. It all seemed possible until we found there were no seed oysters available in Ireland in anything like the quantity necessary to start a real farming business, so it ended up just one of those things that went on and on and nothing ever happened besides the talk and the gathering of information.

It was more than a year after the oysters when I went to Ireland the first time and I sent Donovan a postcard from Belfast. I wrote on it that I was numb with impressions and would tell him all when I returned. I made an asterisk by that line and down on the bottom of the card I wrote "IF." It was a simple stark message and calculatedly so. Donovan didn't know I was in Ireland. He thought I was sitting in an office in New York and here I was writing out a card to him in a post office in Belfast.

As was common in any Belfast building that was a likely target

84

for bombing, I had been searched by a guard at the post office door and all the time I was standing at the counter writing I was thinking that there could be an explosion and I would be killed in the act of composing my cryptic message, which was cryptic not only because I wanted to impress Donovan with where I was, but because I felt, absurdly, that it would somehow be in bad taste to say right out on the other side of the card from the color photograph of Stormont that two days before on Donegall Street six people had been blown to pieces and more than a hundred others had been injured, some terribly. I had the feeling that if I wrote anything so blatant as that the postal authorities would throw the card away. It was as if I was at some resort where the beach was dirty and crowded and there were jellyfish every-where in the water, and though it would be the truth, you would feel badly reporting it openly on a card meant to attract tourists.

When I got back to New York, Donovan said he couldn't under-stand why anyone would want to go to Belfast. He thought it was crazy and irresponsible. "Forget that hell for leather and bound for the North stuff. Those are Socialists up there." I told him that the North was where the historical issues of Ireland were being joined. He said the hell with that. What he wanted to hear about was Dublin and about my visit to my great-grandfather's home and whether or not I'd seen the *Book of Kells* at Trinity.

three

I was talking to the cat when Peter brought the guns up from the basement. I like cats and when one is friendly toward me, like the O'Malley's, which was curled up with its head upside down on the couch beside me, I hold conversations with it. This time, of course, I was doing it purposefully, going out of my way to be casual because of the guns.

The six of us had been waiting in the living room for more than an hour and it was already near one o'clock. Peter's youngest daughter and her overnight guest had been playing "Crazy Eights" at the dining-room table and he didn't want to bring the guns out with the two little girls only a dozen feet away. There was no point in sending them upstairs to bed because the other daughter, the fifteen-year-old, was at the movies and wasn't due back until after midnight, and the guns were going to have to wait until she was home in any case.

We sat around the living room and to pass the time we talked about the pennant race and how it was like old times to have the Yankees back up there again. Whenever anything was said about what was going to happen, it was oblique. Peter and his wife, Sheila, were the only ones I knew well, from the years when he

86

was working in New York and they'd lived a block away and I'd see them at school meetings and parties. I'd looked him up again during the time I was in Boston just to have lunch or to visit their house for dinner. It had nothing to do with Ireland, though knowing that both of them had been born there, I was interested in learning how they felt about the North.

The other three had met me a few times with Peter and they knew I was his friend, but I was not really in with them and I could sense they were reluctant to say too much in front of me. It was one thing for them to think I knew what they were up to and another to have me there with them. There were a couple of guarded references to the "equipment" and Peter told them for Christ's sake they weren't on the telephone now so they could say "guns," because everyone knew that's what was down in the basement, including me, and probably half the neighborhood as well.

Everyone laughed at that and Jimmie Sweeney told him he hoped to hell he was kidding about the neighbors because he didn't want to end up sitting in a prison cell in Fort Worth or someplace while his children grew up and married without a father to advise them.

"Will you listen to him?" Irene said. "As if I was not the one who runs the house and raises the kids. 'Advise them,' he says, and he practically as much trouble as any one of them."

Peter said to leave domestic bickering out of it because it was getting to sound like a marriage counseling session and it was his impression they had gathered together in the service of Ireland.

"Speaking of guns, then," Irene said, "did any of youse hear on the news where some bloody poor soldier was shot today in Belfast?"

"You don't say," said Peter.

"Shoot the whole bloody lot is what I say."

She was a Derry girl, born in the Bogside ghetto and raised in a family that had been IRA from the time of the Easter Rising. The first time I met her there was some talk about the Church and she'd asked me about the changes in the liturgy where I lived and I told her I didn't go any more. "Don't worry, if youse were married to me, you'd be going and make no mistake."

Her accent had been softened by nine years in America but it was still difficult to follow. Though the sound was hard, there was a musical rise and fall to the words that made most of the sentences seem to end with a question mark. She was an attractive woman still, tall and slim and with dark wavy hair and a face that must have freckled easily when she was a child.

There was no Bogside in her husband. He was Boston Irish out of Dorchester: a red-headed man already turning white, though not yet thirty-five, who worked for an insurance company as a claims examiner. He had an aunt still in Kerry and his uncle had been IRA there in the old days and was killed in the civil war, so he knew something of what it was about, but being Irish had never meant that much to him, at least not politically, and without Irene and her family in the middle of it back in Derry and writing to them all the time, he probably would have worn a green tie on St. Patrick's Day and that would have been it.

Burt McAvoy was the other one. When I first met him and got talking about cultural identity and the need for roots, trying to explain myself and the nature of my interest in Ireland, he said his people were all saints, scholars, and horsethieves. Cultural identity didn't interest him. If there had been no trouble in the North, he would have been just another forty-year-old salesman with an Irish name; a personable kidder who saw the humor in everything, including himself and what he did for a living, which was selling electronic equipment for use in refrigerated warehouses. As far as he was concerned, it was a dumb job for good money and he was a natural-born peddler anyway and better that than scissors or encyclopedias.

Burt was sixteen years into his marriage and he and his wife argued a lot about his involvement with Northern Ireland. She thought it was crazy to be mixed up with the cause of slum people who you wouldn't have in your house if they lived in

America; people who loved to drink and fight just to relive the boredom, and who would be lost without an IRA to get excited about. Most of what she'd say was because she was angry at not knowing what he was doing half the time. Like that night. She thought he'd taken the ten o'clock plane on an emergency business trip. That it was a Friday didn't help, but that was what he told her he was doing. Ireland was a more stimulating proposition for Burt than being a salesman or painting over the children's room and putting up the storm windows, and for all his kidding, he was at that stage in life where if he was forced to make a choice, it might well be Ireland that he'd choose and to hell with the wife and the three kids and the refrigerated warehouses.

The O'Malley girl didn't come in until after twelve thirty. She talked with her mother a little about the movie and how the boy who had taken her was all right but she didn't really like him, and then she and her sister and the overnight guest went up to bed and Peter went and got the guns.

That was what we all had been waiting for, but it was different for me because I had not been in on their purchase and was still outside the commitment that accounted for the fact that they were there. To me it was extraordinary that there should be guns bought to kill other men hidden away in a home that was like all the homes of people I knew who were raising families and paying off loans and mortgages and worrying about how things were going in the office.

Peter brought the lot of them up, three under each arm, and set them down in a pile and laid them out evenly on the living-room rug, one above the other. As soon as he started taking them out of the cases, the cat jumped down from the couch and did a purposeful trot over to see what was happening, sniffing around the soft leather of the cases and, busily curious, walking over and around the guns themselves.

Four of them were for hunting, though, as Irene pointed out, anything that can knock down a deer can kill a man, and two were military issue: an Enfield and a Springfield. I only knew the Springfield, and that from Army honor guards, and I went over and picked it up and said that it seemed like old times. I wanted to show I'd been around guns before, that I had some credentials for being there.

The Army was twenty years ago and holding it in my hands again, I was surprised at the weight. The only rifle I'd ever fired, aside from a shooting gallery .22, was the M-1 in basic training when everyone was being prepared to go up on the line in Korea with the Infantry. At twenty-two, basic training was a game. Afterward, when I ended up nowhere near Korea but assigned to garrison duty at an island fort eighteen miles from New York City, we used the Springfield for honor guards and parades. It was an old-time rifle that had been around since the first World War and had won more distance shooting awards than any other. We used to think we were sharp as hell carrying it with white helmet liners on and white puttees and gloves and web belts, and it didn't matter how accurate it was at a distance because we never did any shooting and there wasn't any ammunition on the post.

Peter said to give a look at the Enfield because it could shoot a mile straight, too, and that it had been British military issue for years. "That's the one they like on the other side. One fast shot at a Tommy down the street and take off." He made a quick stiff-fingered move with his hand from the front of his body to indicate a getaway.

Jimmie and Burt brought up the overnight case from the base-ment while I was looking at the guns and talking about my days as a soldier. Peter had gotten it for a dollar at the Salvation Army and it was packed with clips of ammunition and there were two revolvers on top. Burt picked up one of them, a Webley, and handed it to me. "This is the one you want on an assassination job. You shoot a guy in the back of the head with this baby and no one is going to know who he was."

I grimaced to show I was impressed. Holding the gun I felt like

90

a kid on the merry-go-round pretending to himself it was a real horse and he was a cowboy.

"If you don't know who's shot," he went on, "you're going to have a tough time finding out who shot him." I looked at him. He was a salesman with a big expense account and he was talking as if we were both gunmen exchanging professional opinions around a kitchen stove in some tiny adjoining house in the Falls Road in Belfast. I wondered how difficult it would be for him to use the Webley on a man, or for me. Had the real gunmen ever been like us, or were they different?

There was more hard talk like that, about which gun would tear your arm off at how many yards and which would drill you clean and which would blow your chest apart and knock you across the room. All of us were changed by the presence of the guns and what they represented. None of us had ever dealt in violence or risked our bodies in the face of it. Only Irene had been around it and not just read about it or seen it in the movies, and she had never shot anybody or been shot at. None of us, except for her, had ever been physically intimidated in other than a schoolyard sense and it was as if the talk, and the heavy feel of the guns themselves, made us like the men who would use them.

Peter laid them out straight again on the rug and Burt took four Polaroid pictures, photographing three rifles at a time, first from one side, then from the other. Then he took a shot of the revolvers lying on top of the ammunition in the open overnight case. The photos were for identification purposes and were to be mailed to Irene's family to prove the guns had been sent. Jimmie said once they went on their way to Ireland, they could very easily end up in some arsenal in the South where there was no fighting. I told him it might be a little late in the day to do anything about it if all they had were the pictures, but he said at least they'd have something to argue about, and anyway, they could use the pictures first to maybe get some money showing them around to people who were always talking about how they'd be off with the IRA if it weren't for the job and the family.

91

Peter already had one of the guns back in its case and was wiping another clean of fingerprints when Burt asked him why he was bothering with that when there would be plenty of guys handling them in New York. "There'll be prints all over them there."

"I know, but I don't want any of them to be ours. It just makes me feel better."

My prints had to be on the Springfield and the one revolver, and that's all I needed, I thought, to be arrested on a gun-running charge when I was an innocent observer. How could I explain that I was an outsider? And how innocent was I? Did I want to be innocent, even? Certainly not wholly so. I wanted to stand up for Ireland; take small risks in its behalf; be accepted by the hard men. I was glad then that precautions were being taken and that my prints were among those being wiped away and I let myself think that it mattered.

Jimmie and I each grabbed three of the cases and took them out to the car and Peter and Burt brought out the overnight bag with the ammunition. Because the talk about fingerprints was still on my mind, I handled the cases with my fingers and thumb forming a loose fist. We packed them away in the trunk and put a couple of shopping bags with papers in them, Burt's briefcase, and a folded blanket on top of them. The overnight bag went in last.

The moon shone through the leaves of a big twin oak in the yard next door that had branches fanning out thirty yards at least over the street and the car. Everything was gray in the moonlight and I could see the other houses with their trim shrubbery and newly painted shutters very clearly. Peter's was the only house with lights still on.

Irene and Sheila came out and everyone shook hands and Burt and Jimmie and Irene got into the car. Irene was driving the first two hours and she told Peter he was the lucky one because he could go to bed and they were going to be most of the night on the road.

"I don't know about that. I don't think I'll sleep a wink; I'm feeling so guilty that some poor English mother's son is going to get it from the end of one of those mean things you've got packed away there in the trunk."

"There'd better be more than that gets it."

"Ah, you're a hard one, Irene."

Everybody laughed. Irene started the car up and they pulled away from the curb. "See you Monday."

Peter called "God bless" and waved. They drove up to the corner and turned and were gone on their way to New York.

four

When Peter and I first started seeing each other again he was getting anonymous phone calls a couple of times a week. Sometimes there were barroom sounds in the background but mostly there were just the voices, insulting and threatening. "We'll get you yet, you Fenian bastard," and then there would be a click and the line would go dead. "Fuck the IRA." Click. One caller whistled the old Protestant Orangeman's song, "The Sash My Father Wore," and Peter let him go all the way through it and then told him he was a lousy whistler and he hoped he burned in hell.

The phone calls started the night after he was arrested for waving the tri-color flag of Ireland and creating a disturbance in the balcony before a performance by the Scots Guards. It was only a few days after British paratroopers killed thirteen Catholic civil rights demonstrators in Derry and that night was the first time in his life that he had done anything political in the name of Ireland. He had only meant to picket, but he'd never done that either and it didn't seem like much to do once he got there. Burt was with him on the line and he had the flag hidden under his coat, so after a half hour of walking up and down in the cold with strangers, they decided to buy a couple of cheap seats for the performance and take their chances inside.

Once they got to their seats it was a matter of taking a deep breath and then standing and waving the green, white, and orange flag with Peter shouting the old rebel taunts, "Up the IRA" and "Up the Republic," that anyone from Ireland knows. The ushers and the police, who were in the theater because of the picket lines outside and the possibility that something like this would happen, were on top of them almost immediately and all but carried the two of them down the balcony steps with everybody standing and all around that angry murmuring sound of indignation that there should be such a rowdy display with a representative of Her Majesty's Government present in the audience.

The police kidded with them once they had them in the car and told them on the way to the station they were going to put them on the boat to Tooralooraloora Land. For all the kidding, they still booked them and the next day a humorous story about the performance of the Scots Guards appeared in the entertainment section of the morning paper that said a couple of spirited Irishmen with more than a few drops in them had gotten the evening off to a lively start. Somehow only Peter's name and address were carried in the story. For several days he was afraid that someone might try to kill him or beat him up coming out of the house or the office, and he was afraid, too, for Sheila and the children, but he stopped worrying when the calls went into the second week. This was partly because he was surprised and pleased at the kind of celebrity status he had come to enjoy among some of the militant Irish he had never known, and even among business associates and everyday social acquaintances, and partly because, despite all the threats, nothing had happened.

When the story first came out in the paper he was concerned that it might hurt him at work, perhaps even cost him his job, but aside from hearing from his secretary, who had talked to the general manager's secretary, that the general manager had a theory that Peter was trying to do something assertive because he

95

felt inadequate as an Irishman who had missed a chance to be in World War II or the Korean War, the subject was never mentioned.

Peter's father had been a fast gun for Michael Collins in Dublin during the last months of the War for Independence. Before that he had served with Seán Treacy in Tipperary. He was in his seventies and he knew his life was coming to an end and it bothered him to remember some of the people he had killed in those days. More and more when Peter went home to visit, the conversation would turn to that time and Treacy's death and how his father just missed being with him, and Collins' death in Cork in the civil war, and he always told the same story about the night he shot his best friend, who was an informer, and he never told it without saying, "God forgive me."

The friend he had killed had a brother who married and whose sons were about the same age as Peter and were his friends at school and in the scouts. He often saw their father, who was always every nice to him, but whenever he asked after Peter's mother and sisters, he never mentioned his father, and it was not until Peter was in his first year as a scholarship student at University College Dublin that he knew the reason. He was standing on the train platform with his family waiting for the train that would take him back to Dublin and he saw his friends, who were waiting with their parents, and called out to them. The man whose brother Peter's father had killed more than twenty-five years before shook hands quickly with his sons and turned into the station house with his head down so that he would not have to stand on the same platform as Peter's father or risk having to acknowledge his presence.

Nothing was said then but his father wrote Peter a letter some weeks later and told him that during the war it had been necessary to do some things that probably seemed cruel now, and shooting Jimmie Cronin was one of them. Peter never said anything about the letter to the Cronin boys, nor did he ever tell them

96

that he knew his father had killed their uncle. And it wasn't until many years later, when Peter was fully grown and a father himself, and his father was old and frightened of dying, that they talked about it face to face.

After he graduated from University College Dublin, Peter decided to see what America was like. Sheila was a Dubliner, but he never knew her there. They met in New York and married at the end of his first year away from home. They had often visited Ireland over the years since and Peter said he would go back for good if he could get anything like the job he had, but Sheila had come to hate the Church, especially her memory of it growing up, and any discussion of living in Ireland always started an argument. She believed the Irish were a priest-ridden people and she would not expose her children to the guilt and repression she remembered from her convent school days in Dublin. It did no good for Peter to say that even the Church in Ireland had changed, or that their children were already pretty well formed and that it was a little late to impose any more guilt and repression on them than they had already. Sheila did not want to move back to Ireland.

There was a hint of shame at being Irish in her, perhaps because the mark of her speech, the affable brogue that Peter could trade on in business and with male friends, did not achieve the same ends for a housewife and mother in the company of other women and merely made her different from them. If that was so, then it angered her, too, and encouraged a counterbalancing pride for which the troubles in Belfast and Derry came to provide an outlet. "Even if we don't live there, it's our country," she told me one night at dinner. "We own it. And those bastards have been in it for more than three hundred and fifty years and it's time they got the hell out."

Neither one of them had ever had anything to do with politics until Peter was arrested after the flag-waving incident. Up to then being Irish was an occasional booze-up at the local chapter of the Ancient Order of Hibernians, but the Derry killings changed that and once Peter's name was in the paper, he became known to other Irish Americans who wanted to do something for Ireland, and Irene and Jimmie were among them.

Irene had arrived in America the day Jack Kennedy was killed in Dallas and she wondered what kind of country it was she had come to, that she had dreamed would be so marvelous, with the President murdered before she could get off the plane. Her aunt and uncle from Dorchester were at the airport to meet her and she told them she was going back to Derry if that was the way they treated the Irish in America.

She worked for a year as a waitress in a Howard Johnson's and then she married Jimmie and now she was living better than she ever thought she would when she was growing up in the Bogside in Derry. But the Bogside was in her blood, she said, and bad as it was, with nothing to look forward to but spending half your life on welfare, it was God's country and she missed it. She spoke of it as if it were a forest resort by a lake with snow-capped mountains in the distance.

Just before I met Irene, she had flown back home with four revolvers strapped to her body by two belts of ammunition and a pillow tied to the front of her. That was before airport checks became standard practice and she was wearing a maternity dress and was even shown extra courtesies by the stewardesses. One of her brothers was with the Official IRA and had been lifted at Christmastime the year before. She and her mother had visited him at the internment camp at Long Kesh and that was four months after he'd been interrogated and she said it was like seeing a man having a nervous breakdown and trying to hold himself together and pretend he was all right. They had broken his nose and jaw and the fingers on his right hand had been smashed by the heel of a soldier's boot, and there were dozens of small pin scars all over him still from the lighted cigarettes they had put out against his body, but it was the noise machine that made his mind go, so that for a while he was almost crazy.

All Burt knew about Ireland came from what he read in the newspapers and books and from talking to people like Peter and Sheila and Irene. Helping the IRA was the only thing in his life that he seemed to take seriously, and even that he laughed about. But having someone around who can make fun of himself can be important and Burt's sense of humor was very important to Peter during the period of the Ireland for the Irish club.

The Ireland for the Irish club was meant to reflect the sentiments of the men who had occupied the General Post Office in Dublin in 1916, but in a way that would permit participation by those who were against violence but still for a united Ireland. Most of the people who became members were regarding themselves as Irish in a political way for the first time in their lives because of Bloody Sunday and what they were beginning to learn about the conditions under which Catholics had long been living in Northern Ireland, and as a result there was a strong emphasis on civil rights.

There were other more formally established Irish-American organizations whose activities were entirely directed to supporting the fight for civil rights, and there were organizations that supported the two wings of the Irish Republican Army that were conducting the urban guerilla war against the British, but none of the people who belonged to Ireland for the Irish belonged to those other organizations. Theirs was a neighborhood group that started with eight people and grew to thirty-four in the two months and three weeks that it lasted.

Ireland for the Irish was for getting the facts and then exploring the various things that needed doing and deciding together what would be best. At the start, everyone was optimistic about raising money among people with Irish names and they marked up a telephone directory for four towns around and got membership lists from two Irish social clubs in the area. It was agreed that any money that was collected would be distributed equally between the Official IRA, which was Socialist, the Provisional

IRA, which was essentially nationalist and more militant, and the relief fund that had been set up to care for Catholic ghetto children and the needs of displaced families.

It was an ambitious program but a fair one that allowed for the different interests and enthusiasms of the members and in the beginning almost everybody felt a satisfying sense of commitment, a willingness to give of themselves in behalf of a cause.

It was Burt's idea to ask suburban newspapers, the small dailies and weeklies around the area, to write about what they were trying to do and about the plight of Catholics in Northern Ireland. Three papers carried small notices about the club but they weren't interested in writing anything more because they could always run material from the wire services about Northern Ireland if there was room. A local radio show interviewed Irene, who told the interviewer, who usually talked about gardening and beauty tips and recipes, what it was like to grow up Catholic and in an IRA family in the Bogside in Derry. The interviewer said she just couldn't imagine such a world and that it was very interesting for her, and she hoped for all her listeners, too, to have Irene as a guest.

The meetings went well enough for almost two months. Everything was discussed in an orderly manner most of the time and according to parliamentary rules. Three or four of the members took subscriptions to the *United Irishman,* which was the Official IRA newspaper, and Peter got a copy of the Provisional paper, *An Phoblacht,* at a street-corner demonstration he came on by accident on a business trip to Chicago. When Irene came back from her visit home that spring she brought various handbills and pamphlets that described British brutality and the torture of prisoners, and these, along with the papers, were passed around at the meetings and discussed.

At first everyone assumed that the fund-raising efforts among people with Irish names would be more successful if the money was sought for the broad and somewhat ambivalent aim of aid-ing the Catholic poor of Northern Ireland and that nothing should be said about the IRA. It was surprising, therefore, when some of those who made ten- and twenty-dollar contributions said things like, "Put it where it will do the most good," and gave a wink, and the relief of needy children was not what they intended. But most of the people who were called on didn't care at all about Northern Ireland and very few of them gave more than a dollar and most of them gave nothing.

In the two months after the club was formed, it was only able to raise six hundred and fifty-three dollars, and almost half of that came from members. This meant the allotments to the two wings of the IRA and the children's relief fund were far more modest than anyone had expected, and there was a lot of talk at the meetings about the Irish not being anything like the Jews when it came to loyalty to a homeland. It had been a long time, of course, since the Irish had experienced anything even approximating what had happened to the Jews in Europe during Hitler's time, or even the sense of being rejected that went with the day-to-day anti-semitism that had only recently abated in America.

Peter had been elected president because of his action the night of the Scots Guards performance and because he was the kind of man whom people liked easily and who always tried to like everyone else. At forty-two, he was older than most of the other members, and his job was a relatively important one with a well-known corporation, so there was a kind of dignity attached to the idea people had of him. Finally, though he was for the IRA, he had no preference for either wing. However, as each week went by it became increasingly clear to him that there was not going to be enough money to please those who were for supporting civil rights and nonviolent protest and those who wanted to stand shoulder to shoulder with the fighting men. Also, the disagreement between those who were for the Official IRA and those who were for the Provisionals was worsening and the dis-

101

cussions about their respective strategies were growing more heated and parliamentary rules were coming to mean less and less.

Peter felt a stronger man would have been able to impose a discipline on the meetings that he was unable to, but he could understand the various points of view and he was reluctant to seem dictatorial in a group that was voluntarily giving its time for a cause that so few Irish in America seemed to care about. He'd try to kid them out of arguing by saying things like, "Let's get the Six Counties back and then we can fight over how they're going to be run," and that would maybe calm things down for the evening, but then the next week it would start all over again.

It was not until the night that a friend of Irene's brother, who was prominent in the Officials and who was touring America, spoke at one of the meetings that Peter knew the club was not going to last. The visiting IRA man was very impressive and he gave a very stirring account of the background to the conflict with the Unionists in Northern Ireland. He told of the brutalities of the Royal Ulster Constabulary and the B-Specials and the British soldiers, but some members of the club were upset by his frequent references to the goal of a Workers' Republic of Ireland. When he concluded by saying the Provisional bombings were seriously damaging the cause of a United Ireland, the members whose sympathies were with the Provos were offended, particularly the man who had been elected treasurer.

The treasurer had taken his vacation in Ireland the preceding summer and had visited Provisional headquarters at Kevin Street in Dublin. He owned a black IRA beret which he had bought in Ireland and which he sometimes wore to the meetings. Because of the insult to the Provisionals by the visiting Official, who had almost been killed in a gunfight with Provos in Derry the year before, and who had a limp that would last him the rest of his life because of what happened that night, the treasurer wouldn't release the money to pay for his hotel or incidental travel expenses and Peter had to pay the man out of his own pocket.

The real end of the Ireland for the Irish club came at a cookout two weeks later. It was a warm and sunny first Saturday in May and it seemed that it would be a good party despite the bad feeling at the last meeting. Each member was to bring one other person of Irish background or sympathetic to the movement, and though not everyone was able to persuade a guest to come, there were fifty-seven people at the party. At five dollars per person, even with the cost of the whiskey and the food, the profit to the club was more than had been made in any week up to then.

The fact that a doctor and a dentist came with their wives was considered something of a coup because doctors were the sort of people who rarely became publicly involved with anything that appeared to be radical or militant. It was assumed that both were well-to-do and had rich friends as well, and Peter was certain that the club's fund-raising efforts would improve substantially if they could be persuaded to join.

Everything went smoothly at the start and there was Irish music from an accordian and after a while some group singing, and the doctor and the dentist seemed to be having a good time. As president, Peter went out of his way to talk with them and their wives, and in addition to talking about Ireland, he talked about his company and the profitablility of its different divisions and how some new developments figured to affect the price of its stock on the market, and the doctor and the dentist were very interested.

Some of the members arrived late because they had stopped in a bar for two or three drinks first. They were the ones who brought a figure made out of an old suit stuffed with newspapers and hung it from a tree with a sign saying "William Whitelaw, Murdering Bastard." Six weeks before, when Great Britain had imposed direct rule, Whitelaw had been appointed chief administrator for Northern Ireland.

The men who brought the Whitelaw effigy were wearing black berets. They also brought four guns that had been purchased earlier that week. The four guns represented the club's only arms shipment. Two of the guns were to go to the Officials and two were to go to the Provisionals.

Because the cookout was held at the home of a member who lived on the edge of a bird sanctuary, and all around the house there were fields and beyond them woods, they got the guns out of the car and there was a lot of kidding and picture-taking with the guns. One of the men was going around like a British soldier on a street search saying, "All right, luv, up against the wall and legs apart," and Peter told him he was going to have a bowel movement if he didn't point the gun somewhere else. Then a half dozen or so of the men split up with two guns in each group and went off in the woods and played IRA and soldiers.

Peter would have preferred that the guns had never been taken out of the car and he was self-conscious about the picture-taking in front of the doctor and the dentist. He was certain that the real IRA support organizations wouldn't act that way. What really embarrassed him, though, was "the kiddies' matinee" in the woods. There was a lot of laughing about it and remarks about how all men were children at heart, but he knew it looked bad.

The real trouble started after everyone had eaten and the doctor got into an argument with the treasurer and another man about the immorality of violence. The doctor said the eyes of the world were focused on Northern Ireland and that the Catholic community there should be staging one peaceful protest after another and leave it to the Protestant Unionists to be ones who resorted to violence. The cause was a just one and peaceful methods would give it dignity. That's what Martin Luther King had done for the blacks in the South, he said, and someone should be giving that kind of leadership to the Catholics in Northern Ireland.

Someone pointed out that the doctor should have been reading the newspapers from 1968 on and then he'd know how far peace-

104

ful protests got you over there. Peaceful protests were a great way for the Catholics to be massacred out of existence. The arguing spread so that it involved supporters of the Official IRA and the Provisional IRA and eventually there were shouted obscenities and someone called Bernadette Devlin "a Commie whore prostitute" and Irene slapped his face. Bernadette Devlin was a friend of her sister's and practically a saint in her family. The man she slapped told Irene he was going to shoot her in the fucking head if he ever saw her again and she told him that he'd better never go to Derry wearing his black beret because there were some really tough men there and the Provos and Officials both would laugh him off the streets.

Somebody else, not a member but a friend of one of the members who had brought the guns and the effigy of Whitelaw, called the doctor and the dentist and their wives snooty rich bastards who didn't give a fuck about revolution or the working classes. The doctor told him he could take his Irish revolution and shove it and the one thing he was glad of in this world was that he wasn't Irish, and he was only sorry his wife was and had talked him into coming to the crazy party in the first place. He said he thought social justice was the issue, and that when it came to being poor, he knew more about it than anyone there because he'd grown up with immigrant parents who could hardly speak English and lived in a tenement with a toilet on the landing that was shared with another family.

That was the end of the party. Peter and Sheila took Irene, Jimmie, and Burt back to their house and Peter got drunk because he was so mad at having something he thought was useful and important ruined. The cookout had made helping Ireland look ridiculous. What was going on in the North was the most important thing that had happened in Ireland since the Treaty. Men were giving their lives in a fight that had been going on for centuries, and the sense that he was finally a part of it, even in a small way, meant a great deal to him. "All right," he said, "if you don't agree with some of them, don't agree. But don't pretend it's a kids' game or get in a yelling match every time somebody doesn't see it your way."

Irene told him not to take it so seriously and that if he wanted to see some real squabbling he should live a few months in Derry. "Anyway, we're best away from that bunch," she said, "because the way they carry on we'd all be arrested within the month."

That was how they decided to form their own group and do what they could to help the people Irene knew back home. At least they were people with names and addresses and that made whatever they were able to do more real. That all took weeks, though, and during the first four days after the cookout, Peter's right eyelid was twitching and he finally called the doctor who had been raised in the New York tenement and asked if there was a prescription or something that could relieve it. He had a doctor of his own but he wanted to apologize for the fiasco of the party and he told the doctor he was not going to have anything more to do with that group. The doctor agreed that it was a fiasco, but he wasn't interested in hearing more about the Irish or Ireland and he sent Peter a bill for prescribing a drug to relieve his twitching eyelid.

PART III

one

We were on the Slane road for less than an hour when we passed
the Hill of Tara where Laoghaire, Son of the High King Niall,
had sighted the fire from St. Patrick's encampment on the left
bank of the Boyne River in 432. A few minutes later the road
curved down across a stone bridge over the Boyne itself and then
turned sharply uphill past iron-gated old stone battlements. I
asked where the famous battle had been fought that is celebrated
every year by Protestant Orangemen and Terry Keyes said it had
been only a few miles from where we were.

Because the fact that a Protestant army defeated a Catholic
army on Irish soil in 1690 is flaunted still in Northern Ireland, I
thought the site of their victory was near Belfast. Yet if the memory of the Boyne was going to be important, even if it was a defeat
for Catholics, it seemed right that it was close to Dublin. It should
belong to all of Ireland, I thought, and not just to the six counties
of the North where Protestants were obsessed with past victories.
I was for admitting differences and sharing history.

"The whole lot were Danes and Germans and French Hugue-
nots who were fighting with William of Orange at the Boyne that
day, you know," Keyes said. "Or most of them anyway. But the

109

way the Orangemen carry on up there you'd think it was them who beat James II. With their bloody parades and their banners and their marching bands, the bastards."

Driving through Dublin to pick up Keyes earlier that day, Peter and I had gone up Grand Canal Street past Boland's Mill, where de Valera had been in command in Easter Week, and Peter said that was the street the Sherwood Foresters had come down when they tried to break through to the city center during the Rising and the rebels had held them off from positions all around the mill and inflicted over two hundred casualties. It was an ugly, gray warehouse area and I looked at the mill and the canal to our left and the bridges the rebel strongholds had overlooked, and it was easy for me to hear the sound of gunfire and the surprised, angry shouts of British soldiers running for cover over the cobblestone street when they thought all they had to do was to march into town and reinforce the troops surrounding the Post Office the third day of Easter Week in 1916.

In Ireland there were always places where once something happened that is remembered still; where once men fought well or badly; where an informer was executed or a hero hanged; where the famous talked or drank or wrote; where myths were born before history was written, or where the thousands of large and small events occurred that became part of the legend of resistance.

There were monuments in America, and old churches and towers and battlefields, state house steps where speeches were made, and they were all accounted for in guidebooks and were interesting places to see, as a visit to Williamsburg in Virginia is interesting, or as taking the Freedom Bus Ride along the route that Paul Revere rode through the streets of Boston is interesting, but in Ireland the past seemed part of the present, easily remembered or distorted and recreated. It seemed always relevant, and I liked that. I am sure there are Irish who disapprove and think it a national weakness and who say the country is never going to

110

get anywhere until it forgets the past and concentrates on the future, and maybe that is true.

It was Terry Keyes who pointed out the Hill of Tara and told the story of Laoghaire's anger that Patrick's fire should be burning before the Druid fire had been lit, and how he'd sent his men to bring the stranger back to Tara, and how Patrick and his followers had proceeded to Tara chanting the sacred *Faed Fiada* that made them seem to be a gentle herd of deer as they passed by other soldiers of the Druids lying in wait to kill them, and he recited the first verse in Gaelic and Peter translated it for me and said it had for centuries been considered the prayer for the protection of the Irish race.

> I bind me today,
> God's right to direct me,
> God's power to protect me,
> God's wisdom for learning,
> God's eye for discerning,
> God's ear for my hearing,
> God's word for my clearing.

That was supposed to have happened in 432. Of course we were killing time and making conversation on a long drive with three and a half hours still to go, but to talk about St. Patrick and the Hill of Tara was quite different from talking about whatever else might have been happening in the world over fifteen hundred years ago. Ireland was Ireland then and now as well. There had been all the changes and evolvements of fifteen hundred years but the connection was straight. Some have said there never was a St. Patrick, but someone brought the Catholic faith to Ireland and the Hill of Tara was still there to be seen.

Keyes was the Official IRA man who had talked at the meeting of Peter's Ireland for the Irish club when he'd been in the United States on the fund-raising tour the year before. He was a thin, big-nosed man and already broken up around the eyes so that he looked older than we were, though he was only in his late thirties if what he said was true about being twenty at the start of the 1956 campaign. That was when he had joined the IRA for excitement and to prove something to himself. He had been raised to be a nice middle-class boy and he had wanted to see if he had it in him to be IRA. All it meant to him then was men on the run, fighting for Ireland. It was not without some sort of ideological commitment, the way being a priest might seem a worthwhile thing to do if you were twenty, but it was being on the run and tough that really attracted him. I told him that when I was thirteen and fourteen, I'd wanted to join the French Foreign Legion and that the Foreign Legion—"the legion of the lost ones, the cohort of the damned"—had been my IRA.

"It's not the same. I wish I could be polite and say it was, but it's not. I may have been a romantic kid but the IRA was real and not in a North Africa that had been written about in a book fifty years ago. It was the IRA that beat the British and there were men from that time all over Ireland and some of them were active still and I wanted to be like them. The IRA could be a kid's dream but it was something to grow into and with as well. What do you grow into with the Foreign Legion? What has that got to do with anything like building a country?"

I regretted bringing up the Foreign Legion in a car driving to Derry and having it dismissed. It made me feel foolish because it seemed then only to belong to the small classrooms of St. Catharine's parochial school where I'd drawn *Beau Geste* characters in white kepis in the margin of my notebooks. There was a connection, but it was impossible for me to make or argue for it in the presence of a man who had been IRA for seventeen years while I had been riding commuter trains to New York jobs.

That 1956 campaign had dragged on for half a dozen years and had failed badly, but Keyes said he was over being a nice middle-class boy forever because of some of the things that had happened, and that he didn't ever have to prove again that he was a man. "I was shot at enough to do me the rest of my life and I was more than two years in prison and I killed at least one man that I know of and maybe more."

Even though he had been born middle-class, he came from a long line of peasants and in his heart he was a peasant too and proud of his peasant past. The whole of Ireland's history revolved around disputes over the ownership of land and it was the peasants and workers who were going to determine that history now. The main trouble with the great rebellion against the British, he said, was that it had been for middle-class aims. "No one wanted to change the way the country was run. They just wanted to change who ran it. The greatest tragedy of the Rising was losing James Connolly to a British execution squad. He was the one man who knew what the issues were and what the struggle was about. If he'd lived, we'd have had a social revolution as well."

Peter allowed as how that might well be so, going along with him, though Keyes was after all a kind of Socialist and Peter wasn't really interested in that part of it. The fact that we were with Keyes was accidental and due to Irene Sweeney. There was also a certain amount of respectability to the Official IRA because they did less bombing than the Provisionals and had assumed a defensive strategy. People like Peter and me, who were committed to getting ahead in business and living as well as we could, and whose politics were more or less liberal but hardly radical, were inclined to identify ourselves with them because to be on the side of the Provisionals was to have people say to you, "How can you be for an organization that will bomb women and children?", or "How can you be for men who are just plain murderers?" So to be for the Official IRA was to be willing to take a stand on the matter that was defensible at dinner parties and cocktail parties, where no one knew what was going on anyway, except the latest report on the radio or television about someone being shot. I usually avoided saying more than that I was very interested in what was happening and I would agree with anyone who said that what was happening was terrible, because I, too, was outraged by bombings and killings. But really, though I

113

said I was only an observer and tried to tell myself that, I was for the IRA. Maybe I wasn't for urban terror; maybe I couldn't have done any of those things myself; maybe I would have gotten sick to my stomach if I'd seen them done; but even though I wasn't doing anything about it as Peter was, I was on the side of the IRA, the Officials and Provisionals both.

"Let's get up to date," Peter said. "What did your guys think of MacStiofain's hunger strike?"

Seán MacStiofain had been the Provisionals' Chief of Staff and when he was arrested in Dublin that winter he'd gone on a hunger strike in protest against being held for trial. There was an outrageous self-righteousness to it that said he never thought he would be convicted and, when he was sent to prison, he was stuck with a commitment to suicide. Each day the papers reported that MacStiofain had not eaten and even in New York that was news because it seemed possible that he would starve himself to death as Terence MacSwiney had done in Brixton Jail in 1920, and if he had done that it would have been an extraordinary thing. To starve oneself to death for Ireland—and though there were always reasons, some political point to make, ultimately it was for Ireland—had been done by other IRA men, so to declare that he was going to do that was for MacStiofain a serious matter.

It was the priest who was his confessor who finally persuaded him to break his fast by giving him Communion and some broth, and that was the end of it and he started to eat again. I don't know what the priest said or how he argued. He probably told MacStiofain his life was more important to Ireland than his death, or that to commit suicide in this manner would be sinful, particularly with a wife and children. Whatever it was, MacStiofain listened and chose not to die.

Keyes said the Officials thought it was a joke. "He's the only IRA man ever went on a hunger strike and gained weight is what our people say."

Peter and I laughed, enjoying the fact that we were hearing at firsthand the back-biting that went on between the two factions of the IRA. I had no idea what MacStiofain had weighed when he finally came out of prison. He'd been bedridden and seriously ill and what did I know about whether or not he had compromised himself by breaking his fast. All I knew about him was that he had been born John Stephenson in England and there was Irish blood in him and that when he was a young man he had joined the IRA and then at some point afterward he had Gaelicized his name, as Cathal Brugha had done, and others too. But what was extraordinary to me was the idea that an IRA chief who ordered killings would have a confessor and that the Host should be given in a prison hospital to break a commitment to suicide. And that if blood alone was to be the measure, he was probably no more Irish than I.

It was almost four-thirty when we stopped at a pub in Castleblayney and ordered a plate of small sandwiches standing at the bar. Peter and I each had a beer but Keyes ordered an orange soda because he was a Pioneer and had sworn he would never in his life drink alcohol. It was the Irish Christian Brothers who had encouraged him to take the Pledge when he was still a teenager. Peter had gone to them too and they had educated me my first two years of college at Iona and for three unhappy months during the sixth grade when I'd been sent to them, the only new boy in the class.

Keyes, despite his abstinence from alcohol, had no use for them. "You know what the ICB stands for, don't you? International Child Beaters."

Peter said he didn't know about that. "I don't think I'd be anything today if those guys hadn't made something of me. I'd be sitting back in the middle of nowhere pumping petrol. There were good ones and bad ones all right, but I tell you, they cared what you did with your life. The one that hit me the most I still write to."

I nodded. I liked the idea that he felt they were worth his

115

saying it, though I'd hated them when I was a boy. I wished that I could look back on them fondly as Peter did but I couldn't remember a kind word from them or any acknowledgment of my person. All I remembered was the hurt of being hit across the palms with a ruler or slapped on the side of my head for small infractions. I had been taught by women all my life before that; had gone to a progressive public school where each child was supposed to feel that he or she was contributing to the group learning process, and that was not the way you learned with the Brothers. The very fact that they never even called me by my first name seemed harsh to me then. Later, at college, I had liked them, but that was different.

It was strange that those three unhappy months when I was ten years old should be what I had in common with these two Irishmen in a time of revolution. It was almost as if the Brothers were my justification for this ride to the North to Derry.

The only time Keyes had broken his Pioneer pledge was when he had asked for a gin on the plane to America on the fundraising tour, and that was only because he was so terrified of flying and thought it would calm his nerves. "It didn't do anything of the kind, of course, and then afterward I felt terribly guilty."

Peter said he could understand an IRA man going on the dry because that could happen to anyone, but it was a funny thing for an Official IRA man, who was supposed to be a Socialist, to be wearing the Sacred Heart pin of the Pioneers.

Keyes shrugged. "Well, that's the way it started and that's the way it is still. To explain it would take too much time and maybe I couldn't do it even then."

"O.K., but if you were so afraid of flying, why the hell didn't you take a boat?"

Keyes told him he couldn't afford to lose the time and anyway, he didn't want the people on the other side who were paying his way to know how he felt about planes. "For Christ's loving sake,

116

man, how much money do you think I'd have gotten if they knew I was afraid to ride in an airplane?"

I offered cigarettes around, as one learns to do in Ireland, and a small, red-faced man at the end of the bar went out to his car and brought in a medicine bottle half filled with poteen and pushed it surreptitiously into my jacket pocket. Poteen is Ireland's famous illegal alcoholic beverage that is made in country stills. The man waved away my thanks and said he wished there'd been more to give me. "Drink it in good health and with a bit of milk when you're back in America and remember you were here in Castleblayney."

A race meeting from England was on the television and a horse named Brown Lad won and I told Peter I hoped that it was an omen of the good things that were to come.

"You've got a pocket full of poteen already. I don't know how much better you want it."

"That poteen will drive a man daft," Keyes said.

We went over the border into Northern Ireland at Aughnacloy, passing first the Irish Gardai in their navy blue, silver-buttoned overcoats and broad crowned caps, and then inched our way across the raised ramps that had been built into the road to discourage machine gunners and grenade throwers in speeding cars, past the Customs shed to the British checkpoint. A half dozen soldiers stood around an armored personnel carrier and they made us get out and open the hood and trunk of the car.

"Do we look like bombers to you?" Peter asked as they searched the car.

"You never know until you've caught one, now do you, sir," the sergeant said.

Sheep and cattle spotted rolling fields that were divided by hedgerows into rectangles and triangles and huge squares. Although the fields along the road through Tyrone were as green as I remembered the fields the year before riding the train to

Belfast, and the trunks and bare branches of the trees were green and thickly ragged with ivy, it was a chill gray end of winter day with no suggestion of spring to it.

After what Keyes had said about being afraid of planes, we had been talking about fear. Not specific, sensible fear, but things the idea of which frightened you. Keyes said that aside from planes he had always been afraid of something happening to his eyes and that when he was doing jobs in the 1956 campaign and they'd be out in the country at night, that was the one thing he worried about. "Any time a branch would slip back from the man in front of me and brush across my face, even softly, I'd have to fight myself not to cry out and give us away. I tell you the truth, I think the Army could get anything out of me if they tied me to a chair and said they were going to blind me."

Peter said he didn't think he'd be much good under interrogation and that he had to hand it to the guys who had taken it and not broken down.

"There's always some who break down," Keyes said. "Not everyone is the same, you know. You've got to expect that. A man's lifted who really knows something, like where an arms dump is, we don't take the chance. We move it." He stopped and picked at his tooth with his thumbnail a few seconds and looked out the car window. Then, still looking away, he said, "You know, one of the worst things when they're working you over and you're disoriented and hardly know who you are or why, is to have some soldier act friendly to you. That's a terrible thing. You want so to believe he means it. You're so goddamned vulnerable by then you could almost cry at a show of kindness and it's just part of the routine."

Peter said he'd read somewhere that a writer on a British paper, when all the stuff had come out on the torturing, had said it wasn't really torture at all but barracks room brutality, like they were just cuffing guys around and the Irish couldn't take it.

"Ballocks to that. Let the bloody bastard go through it and then write about it. There's a lot of Irish men aren't ever going to be the same again. And a lot of them are poor bastards who had nothing to do with anything."

I told him that all of it scared me but that I could especially see what he meant about his eyes. "Just being tied to a chair would about do it for me," I said. "Forget the other about the blinding. I'd probably cave in the first time they hit me and tell them everything I knew and some things I didn't."

I was surprised that he was talking the way he was to us, who had been through nothing, and I felt it necessary to make clear that I was in no way his equal; that I had less capacity to control my fears than he did. I wondered, too, if he had ever been broken, perhaps by a show of kindness.

two

The Rossville Flats is a ten-story apartment building that dominates the new housing development that has been built up for the Catholic poor of the Bogside in Derry. There are other tall buildings in the development, but most of them are not more than three stories high and they are set around open concrete walkways and play areas which had undoubtedly seemed beautiful in the architect's sketches, and which are better by far than the rows of dirty gray adjoining houses that had stood in that place since the turn of the century, except that, new though the development is, it already has the tacky, not quite substantial look of the modern apartment housing that has been built for blacks of Harlem and Bedford-Stuyvesant in New York.

The Bogside lies just beyond the great walls of the old city of Londonderry, which is the official designation still because early in the seventeenth century it had been part of a large land grant obtained by the City of London and settled by English Protestants and Scots Presbyterians. In 1689, the year before the Battle of the Boyne, Londonderry withstood a siege by Catholic forces under James II for a hundred and nine days until the food ship *Mount-*

joy broke through the great chain across the River Foyle and relieved the Protestant garrison.

To Catholics it is Derry still and the ninety-foot-high pillar honoring the Rev. George Walker, the Presbyterian minister who had been Governor during the famous siege, has been blown up by bombers of the Provisional IRA. Queen Elizabeth's deputy, Mountjoy, to whom the great Gaelic chief, Red Hugh O'Neill, surrendered in 1603, gave his name as well to the prison in Dublin where the eighteen-year-old IRA volunteer, Kevin Barry, was hanged by the British in 1920.

It was the annual Protestant celebration of the lifting of the Siege of Londonderry that marked the beginning of the current troubles in Northern Ireland. There had been violent reactions to Catholic civil rights demonstrations during the preceding year, but it was the parade of 15,000 Protestant marchers on August 12, 1969, which provoked the five days of rioting that left nine dead and five hundred Catholic homes burned out in Derry and Belfast.

"Youse want to see what it's like to live in an up-to-date slum?" Kevin Maguire asked us that first morning when he'd taken Peter and me over to the Bogside Inn for a "tincture" to start the day with. "Youse want to see what we have to be thankful for?" He made a quick move ahead of us and walked backward for a couple of steps with his arms outstretched. "Don't believe what youse read about Catholics in the Six Counties being mistreated." He did a little strut back to us. "We live like kings."

Kevin Maguire was Irene Sweeney's younger brother, a kidder with thick, reddish muttonchop sideburns, and we were staying with him and his mother. There was an older sister, Kathleen, who lived in the Rossville Flats itself with her husband and four children. Her husband was a welder who hadn't worked in almost three years. They were both in their early thirties and looked older. Kevin was twenty-three and had worked a total of

121

nineteen months since leaving school at fifteen. The other brother, Joe, had a wife and seven children who lived about a mile away up in the Creggan Estates, another new development for Catholics on the edge of the City Cemetery. Joe was the oldest and the one who had been in Long Kesh and he was only out a few months and not right yet. He had no job either. All of them were "on the brew" because employment opportunities were scarce and most jobs paid poorly. A married man with children could make more money on welfare, with the family allowance and free milk and meals at school, and the free medical and dental care, than he could if he was working. Both Kevin's mother and sister had been on the rent strike for more than two years, but as the Government owned the housing development, it accounted for part of its lost rental income by withholding the family allowance from Kathleen at least, and others like her, without risking further provocation of the rebellious Catholic community by forcing protesting families to move out.

It is regrettable that the urban poor of the world sometimes spoil the new living environments that have been created for them, marring with their own dirt and scrawlings surroundings that were meant to be beautiful and uplifting. The environment around the Rossville Flats was marred by crude black crosses painted on the pavement of the open walks to mark the spots where the thirteen Catholic civil rights protesters died on the afternoon of January 30, 1972, which was Bloody Sunday. On the sides of some of the buildings there were deep saucer-like holes that a man could put his fist into. They had been made by bullets from the high-velocity rifles the British soldiers of the First Parachute Regiment were firing that day. And everywhere—on the pavements, on the fences, on the buildings, in the stairwells and along the hallways, and scratched even on some of the apartment doors—there was the defiant graffiti of the Catholic poor. There were no obscenities, nor were there any drawn hearts or names of boys and girls who thought they were in love, and there were none of the standard, sometimes amusing observations on the human condition that one sees on subway platforms and in public washrooms. But several hundred times, several thousand times, perhaps, there were written assertions such as JOIN THE IRA, PROVOS RULE, INFORMERS BEWARE, UP THE OFFICIALS and THE GREAT SEEM GREAT BECAUSE WE ARE ON OUR KNEES—LET US RISE.

Because of the state of mind revealed by those Catholic graffiti and the four years of violence that had created it, and because the upper stories of the Rossville Flats overlooked the whole of the Bogside, there were British soldiers on duty in the long open hallway on the top floor twenty-four hours a day.

It was almost two in the morning when Kevin Maguire and I left his sister's place in the Flats. We'd been sitting talking over tea and bread after the bars had closed. We'd just crossed Rossville Street and were entering Glenfada Court to go to his mother's apartment when a voice shouted out of the darkness about thirty yards to our right.

"Hey youse sojers up there. You know what? One of your fucking mates got himself shot in the fucking face tonight. And now he hasn't got a fucking nose."

Then there was another, younger sounding voice. "Youse hear that? No nose to smell the fucking flowers with any more."

Then the first voice again. "How do you like that, youse fucking whores? We got another one of youse bastards and one of these nights we're going to fucking well get youse."

When the first voice shouted out of the darkness, I felt a sudden tingling of fright throughout my body because it was so unexpected a sound and it was late and the two of us were walking alone, and then because it was so cruelly threatening, so full of hate, and I was afraid it was somehow directed at me.

I had spent the evening drinking and talking in various bars with the people of the Bogside. I had played the guitar and we had sung songs together and I had even sketched a portrait of a Provisional officer for his girl and then two young volunteers at another table had asked me to sketch them and I'd gone over and they had bought me drinks and I'd drawn their pictures too. I'd been accepted; I'd ingratiated myself with the Catholic poor and with members of the Provisional IRA; yet the rough, angry sound of the voices set me apart again and suddenly made me feel I was an object, like the soldiers, and like the soldiers, an intruder.

Just as suddenly I sensed myself an object to the soldiers too. Two men walking alone in the Bogside at that hour had to be suspicious any night, but this night there were voices shouting for British blood.

"Let's move, for Christ's sake," I said to Kevin.

"No. Just walk normal. Youse start to run and the'd be sure it was us."

There were another forty yards to go before the walkway turned so that we'd be protected from the view of the soldiers by the corner of one of the smaller apartment buildings. We walked normally for those forty yards and all the way I felt as if I had no clothes on. Just as we made the turn there was the sound of running feet coming toward us from the darkness ahead and I thought, "Oh my God," and the fear started again, and then there was a loud whisper, "Hey, Kevin, is that youse?" and two figures came up to us from the darkness and waited to walk along beside us.

"Was that youse scaring the poor sojers and all the wee 'uns and their mas as well?" Kevin asked.

"Don't tell us we scared youse too."

"Youse bloody well did. I thought they were going to start fucking shooting and it was us who was out there in the open. They could have drilled us easy."

"They'd have to think youse was a fucking ventriloquist. We was nowhere near youse."

"That's going to stop them I suppose?"

"Ah, you'll be on the nerve pills next. Who's your mate?"

Kevin said I was a Yank friend of his sister Irene in America and the two of them nodded at me and I nodded back. I felt secure again. Being with Kevin Maguire made me acceptable to these

124

two teenagers who were no older than my sons. But I was worried still that the soldiers would come and find us; that the soldiers up on the roof had contacted their headquarters and some patrol would be out in armored cars to pick us up. I wished we were inside the apartment.

We were near the door of Kevin's mother's building by then and there was an overhead light. I could see that one of the boys had the tousled-haired tough look of a Dead End Kid, a young Billy Halop or Gabe Dell. The other wore his hair long, almost to his shoulders, and had wolf eyes in a pock-marked face.

"America?" the Dead End Kid said. "I wish I was there and not in this fucking place. Why'd youse come here for?"

I told him I was very interested in Ireland and that I'd come to see what was up and that I'd been over the year before.

"Well, when youse go back this time, tell President Nixon to tell his pal Heath to get the fucking sojers out. Or better, tell him to send us some guns and we'll blow the bastards out ourselves."

I told him it wasn't likely that Nixon would listen to anything I said and then there was a long pause and I tried to think quickly of something funny and appropriately scornful I could say about Nixon and the situation in Northern Ireland. Kevin turned to go. "Well, up the Stickies," he said.

"Stickies" was the slang term for the Official IRA because the traditional IRA Easter Lily paper badges they sold had glued backs that could be moistened like a stamp and stuck to the lapel of a jacket. The lilies commemorating the 1916 Rising are like the poppies that are still sold in America around Memorial Day except that they are little pieces of flat paper colored orange, green, and white. The badges the Provisionals sold had no glue and a straight pin was needed to fasten them on. For a time, because of that, the Provisionals were called "Pinheads," but that never caught on the way "Stickies" did.

I had bought a Provisional badge from a man who was selling them from table to table in a bar earlier in the evening and was wearing it pinned to the collar of my wool shirt. Peter had bought one too, as had Kathleen, who was more Provo than not, but Kevin had refused because he said it was against his principles. Everyone in the Bogside knew he was for the Officials, he said, and he'd be a hypocrite to buy a Provisional badge.

"Fuck the fucking Stickies," the boy with the long hair said. "What are youse all doing any more? Not a fucking thing."

"We've done plenty."

"Not fuck all so far as I can see."

"Youse and your bloody Provo toughs. Yelling at the sojers in the dark."

"Tougher than youse Stickies, youse can bet. The fucking sojer got shot, didn't he?"

"If he did, it wasn't youse two who done it."

"Never mind who done it. It wasn't a fucking Stickie shot him."

"We shot our share."

"Fuck you did."

"You know we did."

"Listen," the Dead End Kid said, "any time youse Stickies want to stand up for Ireland, we'd be glad to have youse with us."

That was the conversation: all banter about killing and revolution, as if they were fans of rival football teams kidding with each other before the big game. We said good night and Kevin and I went upstairs to his mother's apartment. On the stairs I asked him if the two boys were really Provos and not just sympathizers.

"Maybe they are and maybe they're not. All they had to do was know about the sojer getting shot. And maybe that didn't happen even." He told me how he had seen one who had been shot by a sniper and while they were carting him away dead on a stretcher with a tarpaulin over him, his beret lying ten yards from where he was hit, with blood and brains on it, children were making up a song about it. "They were actually singing about his brains being all over the place while the other sojers were carrying him to the truck. What I mean is, we all hate the sojers and a lot of

126

times youse do things just to get at them, don't youse know. They're such bastards, even though they're working class themselves, and youse want to scare them or do anything youse can to them. So maybe one was shot tonight and maybe he wasn't."

The lights were still on in the living room and the couch was opened up and Peter was asleep in his clothes on the inside half with a couple of blankets over him. There was no heat left in the coals in the grate and it was almost as cold in the room as it was outside. I sat down on the open side of the couch and lit a last cigarette and looked at the room. It would have fit three times into my living room at home. The fireplace wall across from me was painted orange and the other walls were blue and the ceiling was yellow. A heavy-framed, brown-tinted picture of the Sacred Heart of Jesus that was too big for the room was over the fireplace and statues of the Virgin Mary and St. Joseph stood on top of the television set alongside a crucifix. There was another large, almost church-sized statue of the Virgin in the corner on the other side of the window.

On one of the narrow walls by the entryway into the kitchen there was a picture of Pádraic Pearse, who had read the Proclamation of the Republic aloud in front of the General Post Office in Dublin on Easter Monday to launch the Rising. A large wood-beaded rosary from Lourdes hung on the other. Above the sofa was a framed newspaper page of portraits of Republican heroes starting with the men who had signed the Proclamation and including others who had been executed or who had died on hunger strikes. Cathal Brugha was one of them, but there were no pictures of those who had accepted the Treaty and taken the side of the Free State, so Collins was out and so was deValera.

There was a cuckoo clock that sounded every hour and an old-fashioned color print of Grecian columns and blue mountains and an early evening orange sky, and photographs of the two married Maguire girls in their wedding dresses, but the statues and the rosary and the picture of the Sacred Heart and the Republican portraits defined the room and the people who lived in it.

Old Mrs. Maguire had told us that morning she didn't care whether a boy was Provisional or Official as long as he was willing to fight for Ireland. She had stickers on every window of her apartment that said WE SUPPORT THE IRA. "I don't know what's wrong with the people of the Bogside these days," she'd said when she brought us some tea before we'd gone out for breakfast. "I think half of them are Unionists at heart the way they bow and scrape to the soldiers. You'd think Bloody Sunday never happened. They tell me that up in the Creggan some of the girls are even going to Army dances and doing Lord knows what afterwards."

Then she'd given Peter and me booklets about the Blue Army of Our Lady of Fatima. "It's not violence that's going to destroy the world," she'd said. "It's sex and alcohol. And the good Lord knows we've got enough drunkenness right here in Derry. It's all there in the booklet. You can read it for yourselves."

She'd pulled her sweater-jacket tight across her front and gone back to the kitchen in a *that's that and I've done my duty* kind of way. It was old-lady amusing when she said it but it was crazy to think like that: that violence was all right but sex was bad. As for the drunkenness, well there were a lot of things that could make that happen, and no sex or bad sex was probably one of them. And no work was another. Still, I thumbed through the booklet and read passages from it to please her and remembered my own mother and her devotion to Our Lady and all the novenas she'd made and the madonna collection she had in the big glass case in the hall. And I remembered, too, all the penances I'd said after confession in front of the Our Lady altar.

That was in the morning and now it was late and I was smoking and wondering what it would be like to be one of those soldiers on sentry duty on top of the Flats and hear voices coming at me out of the dark, knowing that someone like myself, perhaps a friend, had been killed or maimed by the voices, and that they were waiting to kill me too.

Dozens of movies and books and poems by Kipling that I could still recite had taught me to admire British soldiers. They had fought with Wellington and had been Tommy Atkins all over the world in the days of Empire. There was Kitchener and the Sudan and Harry Faversham redeeming the four feathers. There was the Eighth Army and "Lily Marlene" and beating Rommel at El Alamein. On horseback they'd charged with the Light Brigade and in the air they'd "diced with death" and defeated the Luftwaffe. Yet the men who patroled the streets of Derry and Belfast, rifles at the ready, hard and remote and efficient in camouflage fatigues bloused over their boots and big-collared flak vests, were no heroes to the people with whom I had chosen to identify. I was on the side of the Fuzzy Wuzzy and the forces of the Mahdi now. I was standing with the cannoneers at Balaklava.

I lit another last cigarette and thought about Captain Flagg at the end of *What Price Glory* saying that the profession of arms was like a religion. But what did that have to do with me? I was for peace and love. I was a reasonable, decent, compassionate person who properly believed that war was an insanity and that to be responsible for the suffering and death of one's fellowman was immoral and inhumane. What did I know about soldiering? During my two years of garrison duty my uniforms were all tailored and my shirts were pressed with three military creases down the back and two down the front and you could see the sky in the shine of my shoes. What kind of soldier was that?

Maybe, at bottom, it was the idea of authority that impressed me: that things are, should be, a certain way, and that those who insure that, as soldiers are meant to do, are to be respected. Maybe it was that I was still disposed to allow that the basis of power was right, and that made a part of me always respectful of priests and police officers and judges and gray-haired men in dark expensive suits. And soldiers, too, because they represented the ultimate power of the state.

What about the IRA? They were rebels. They were political renegades and desperados. They went against the way things were. Well, I was for that too. Except you could argue that they were absolutists as well, or a lot of them were. You could argue that Pearse reading the Proclamation in front of the Post Office was the Pope speaking *ex cathedra;* that the Proclamation was their sacred writ. Well, they were dreamers too. And some were just fighting men, pure and simple.

It was like peeling an onion. The IRA was a lot of things and so was the Army. And authority wasn't the issue. What were those authority figures representing the ultimate power of the state who were stationed on top of the Rossville Flats but young men who had joined the Army to get away from the confines of home and the prospect of boring jobs or no jobs at all? The Army was their opportunity to see something other than factories and mills and the neighborhood faces they'd known all their lives in some bleak working-class town in England that was not so different from Derry or Belfast. The Army was their chance at excitement and danger to test their ideas of manhood. Now that they were combat soldiers in a civil strife, they were clearly something different from what they'd been.

And where did that lead but back to the idea that the profession of arms was like a religion. I was back to Captain Flagg and the outfit moving up on the line again at Belleau Wood. It had nothing to do with the ultimate power of the state. What attracted me was the fact that they had no choice, given what they were, but to go. Because what did it matter that the soldiers on top of the Flats came from somewhere else, had young brothers or sisters at home in Manchester or somewhere? What did it matter that they had played on their school rugby teams and collected Beatles records, or if one of them had a sick mother or a father who drank too much and lost money he couldn't afford betting the horses. The role of British soldier came first in the order of being, for me in experiencing their presence and for them in projecting it. Anything else was for fooling around the barracks or for home leave. If they didn't feel that way, let them become clerk typists or cooks or join the motor pool. Let them leave the Army.

It was after three o'clock in the morning and I was sitting up alone in an Irish Republican household in Derry, wearing a Provo Easter Lily pinned to the collar of my shirt, and arguing with myself about the way a soldier should be. I was trotting out all my romantic ideas about fighting men and about authority and about role playing, and I was analyzing the situation and making my insightful insights. Maybe it was the fear that had done it. Maybe being afraid had sprung something loose in my head as if I was drunk. I could have been killed by one of those soldiers. It wouldn't have mattered where he came from or what his memories were of kitchen suppers with the family. One of them could have responded to the threats of the shouting by putting a bullet into my back. "You say you shot the face off one of my mates? Well here's a shattered backbone for one of you then." Those things happened. I could have been killed as an Irish rebel, shot down in the Bogside with my Easter Lily badge on my collar.

The next day I was walking up the dirty semi-open stairwell of the Rossville Flats with Kevin's sister, Kathleen. We were going to her apartment and at the second level we passed some children on their way up to the top to see the soldiers.

Most of the eight- and ten- and twelve-year-old boys in the Bogside threw stones at the soldiers when they drove through their streets in patroling armored cars, but to many of the very small children the soldiers with their guns were an exciting presence and seeing them was what seeing soldiers has always been for small children.

One of the little boys on the stairs could not yet have been four. He was small and round-faced with cheeks so pink they almost seemed rouged and old-fashioned steel-rimmed glasses. He couldn't climb the steps fast enough to keep up with his two friends and I carried him the remaining flights to the top be-

131

cause I wanted to be a good fellow who was friendly to children.

There were three of them on duty. It was late in the afternoon and it did not figure that they were the ones who had been up there the night before. One stood facing the door to the roof with his rifle at the ready and the other two were staring out over the railing at the Bogside. One of them, a young man with a moustache to look older, turned to look at us. I was carrying Peter's camera on a strap around my neck and Kathleen said why didn't I take a picture of the boys with one of the soldiers. She nodded toward the one with the moustache and he reached out with his hand and pulled the little boy with the glasses over in front of him. The other two boys hung back, shaking their heads. The young soldier assumed a soldier pose, standing straight with his head back and a self-conscious smile on his face, his rifle held at his side, his left hand on the little boy's shoulder, and, still breathing heavily from the climb, and from carrying the boy, I snapped the picture of the two of them together.

Except for the rifle, it was almost the same pose as a picture that had been taken of me with a sailor named Jack when I was five years old. The sailor was a nephew of my grandmother's neighbor and when the fleet was in New York it was arranged for us to visit him so I could see the battleship *Louisville*. A keepsake photo was taken of me standing in a short-sleeved, wide-collared, white summer shirt in front of the ship's big forward guns and the sailor, Jack, was standing behind me with his hands on my shoulders.

That was in mid-Depression and I never saw or heard of Jack again. I used to look in the papers for news of the *Louisville* during the war and I'd wonder if he had been killed. If he survived the war and the years after, he is probably in his sixties now and waiting for retirement, but because I kept that snapshot for years, the memory of him as he looked that day is still exact enough so that if it was 1934 again and the *Louisville* was in port, I could go aboard and find him.

The little boy in the steel-rimmed glasses never saw that picture of himself with the young, moustached British soldier. I didn't know who he was and I'd only taken it to account for our being on the roof.

Going back down the stairs, the other boys pushed him against the wall and told him he was a dirty traitor for having his picture taken with the "sojer" and the little boy started to cry. Kathleen pulled the other two back, as any mother or schoolteacher would, shaking her finger at them and telling them to leave the little one alone because he didn't mean anything bad and it was the Yank who wanted the picture and not him.

We went on down the stairs and I was holding the hand of the boy who had cried. He was still sniffling and rubbing his nose with the back of his other hand, and Kathleen said, "The Limey bastards. I wish it was a gun youse had on him and not just a bloody camera."

three

Gerry Fallon, Kathleen's husband, the welder who had not
worked in three years, a big-faced man with tight curly hair that
was more gray than brown, told me I was so dark around my eyes
that I looked like a raccoon.

"You need some kip time," he said. "If you're off to Donegal
tonight, you'd better grab some kip time in the kids' room."

I was tired from the late nights and from not being able to sleep
on the couch in the morning with Mrs. Maguire up and around
her small apartment by seven-thirty, and that night we were to
drive over to Donegal to see Peter's retired bartender friend from
Boston.

Kathleen took me into the children's room and it was like a
small barracks with twin beds and two cribs. The linoleum on
the floor was buckled and broken away. There was a white
painted bureau with a statue of the Blessed Mother on it squeezed
into the corner and a tinted print of the thorn-encircled Sacred
Heart of Jesus over one of the beds. I lay in my clothes on top of
the bed next to the window and Kathleen said to pull the comforter over me and she'd wake me at seven.

I was wearing a woolen shirt and a fleece-lined leather jacket and still I could feel the damp chill from the walls, and even the comforter seemed damp and cold on top of me. I lay quiet and tried to let my mind go free so I could sleep but instead I thought how remarkable it was that I was there. At home I had a wife and three teen-aged children and two cars and a cat. The apple tree next to the kitchen was probably going to fall down on my house if something wasn't done about it soon.

What time was it there? My watch said five-sixteen. That meant it was just past noon at home. My sons and daughter were at school and my wife was probably cleaning up the house or out shopping or on the phone to her sister.

We had lived in that house for a dozen years and it was part of me all right, but they were doing what they were doing and it had nothing to do with me now or with where I was.

There weren't any apple trees where I was and the only car was Peter's, and that was rented from the South. That had nothing to do with the way these people lived. These were the poor of Derry in Northern Ireland. I was insurance- and mortgage-poor from living in the suburbs of New York, which was nowhere near the same thing.

Well, there were plenty of poor at home if that's what I wanted. I didn't have to travel to Northern Ireland to find the poor. But if it was the Bronx or Brooklyn and there was no Ireland to talk about and no discrimination against Catholics to resent, what would I know of people like these? What would we have in common with no history and no heroes and no idea of the eight centuries of resistance to define them for me?

Forget home. I hadn't come to Derry to think of home. I was lying on a strange child's bed, cold in all my clothes, smelling the damp brackish smell of the room, three thousand miles away from that.

Outside the window was the open walk area of St. Joseph's Place and beyond it, the waste ground where the Saracens loaded

135

with paratroopers had come roaring and weaving through the crowds on Bloody Sunday the winter before, so I thought about that.

When Bloody Sunday happened, it was eleven in the morning at home and I was probably drinking coffee in the dinette and reading the book section or the entertainment section of *The New York Times*. And right outside that window and all around the building and across the street, hundreds of people like Kathleen and Gerry Fallon and Kevin Maguire and others whom I had met in the bars, had been running, terrified, trying to find a place to hide, because it wasn't just gas or rubber bullets, it was live rounds; and the paratroopers weren't just firing over their heads to scare them and restore order, they were killing people.

It had been a sunny, mild day for mid-winter and the afternoon had started with a march organized by the Northern Ireland Civil Rights Association to protest internment of suspected IRA men without trial or even formal charges. It was a large-scale demonstration in civil disobedience and more than fifteen thousand Catholics from all over Northern Ireland took part. The march stretched out for over six hundred yards and it took an hour to reach the Army's barbed-wire barricade at William Street, a quarter of a mile from the center of the city, where the stone throwing began.

Stone throwing was the standard expression of the people's anger against authority in Derry and a predictable response that day to the Army's presence at the barricade. It was a form of hooligan war that the soldiers knew how to contain and there were usually limits to the hurt that could be inflicted by either side. Sometimes the hurt was severe because when the Army retaliated with rubber bullets at short range, they could break a leg or shatter a jaw. A hit with a broken piece of pavement could be just as damaging, but the soldiers were protected by Plexiglas face masks that turned down off their helmets and big Plexiglas shields and flak jackets and knee and shin guards. The people had no protection against the six-inch rubber bullets or the water cannon or the CS gas other than the fact that they could usually run away from a confrontation more easily than the soldiers could.

There were thousands of soldiers on duty all over Derry, but the ones who came down into the Bogside and did the killing that day were paratroopers. Everyone knew that the paratroopers, with their red berets and their nine-year enlistments, were the cream of the British Army. They were the real professionals, the elite fighting men, the really mean bastards that you sent in to take the hard terrain in a war, not to control a crowd of angry stone throwers in a civil disturbance. You didn't need paratroopers for a street mob.

The march was supposed to end with speeches at the Guildhall on the other side of the wall in the business center of the city, but it never got there. Only a few hundred marchers had reached William Street when the officer's voice came over the loudspeaker: "You may not come through this barricade." That's when the stone throwing started, and the Army retaliated with purple-dyed water from the water cannon and CS gas. The crowd was sullen and confused and some were afraid as word spread that an old man and a boy had been shot. Then there was the roaring sound of the Saracen armored personnel carriers weaving in through the people milling around the Rossville Flats.

The paratroopers weren't wearing their distinctive red berets when they emptied out of the carriers, their faces blackened with pigment. They had steel helmets on with the Plexiglas masks turned back on top to give them a clear view for shooting. The stone throwing was over. The paratroopers hadn't been brought in for that. They were there to take on the IRA. It didn't matter that neither the Officials nor the Provisionals were around to fight. They expected to have it out with the IRA, and in the tough euphemism of the military, they were going to bloody its nose.

Kathleen Fallon saw a balding, middle-aged man in a dark blue quilted car jacket run across Rossville Street toward the crowded semi-open stairwell we had just climbed with the chil-

137

dren and where, that day, she was flattened out on the stairs with scores of other people who were crawling over one another trying to get to the upper floors. Just as the man reached the building, his face disintegrated from a high-velocity bullet that a paratrooper fired into the back of his head.

Each time a bullet rang off the metal bars that crossed over the open areas of the stairwell there would be muffled curses and cries of fright and Kathleen prayed she wouldn't be killed and that her children were safe inside the apartment and that her husband was not among those who had been shot. But even with her eyes closed tight and the noise of the gunfire and the screaming, there was the image of what had happened to the man's face inside her head.

All that time Gerry Fallon was crouched by one of the low apartment houses across Rossville Street. He watched an armored car track a girl in a maroon coat, the armored car like a big steel slug, except that it could move much faster than the girl realized and it ran her down, knocking her into the air with her coat and dress flying up and her legs kicking and Fallon saw a flash of white underwear and then she was a crumpled pile of maroon cloth in the street.

He saw a priest crawl out to give the last rites to a man while bullets ricocheted off the pavement around him and then a boy waved his arms and screamed, "Shoot me. Shoot me. Don't shoot the priest," and the soldiers shot him and the boy fell and someone grabbed at his legs and dragged him away.

There was a teen-aged boy with Fallon, and another man who had been wounded in the thigh sat on the ground with his belt tied tightly as a tourniquet around his upper leg. A spinster who lived with her married sister on the floor above the Fallons was huddled down beside them crying hysterically, "They're going to kill us all. They're going to kill us all."

A paratrooper backed around the corner of the building, firing across the street as he came. He turned his head and saw them and spun around with his rifle on them and shouted, "Move and you're dead." It was possible, with the noise of the shooting and the screaming of the people all around them, that he had said, "Move *or* you're dead," and that what he meant was for them to get out into the street, and Fallon almost cried out to him to please say it again so that he would know what to do, when the paratrooper ordered them up against the wall of the apartment building with their hands on top of their heads. The boy beside Fallon grabbed at the barrel of the paratrooper's rifle, trying to turn it away and run, but the paratrooper was a grown man and stronger and he jammed the rifle into the boy's stomach and fired it and part of the boy's back came away with the blast.

Fallon and the woman stood with their faces pressed against the brick wall and the man with the tourniquet around his thigh sat with his back against the wall and his hands clasped on top of his head, mumbling prayers in Latin. The woman was sobbing with her mouth open and her face puffed and wet from crying, the saliva and mucus hanging down in thick strings from her nose and chin, and Fallon was certain, with the boy lying dead behind him, that he would never live to see his family again.

When the shooting was over the paratroopers rounded up several groups of men who had not been able to get into the apartment houses and Gerry Fallon was one of them. This was the second phase of the operation that was to have begun with taking on whichever wing of the IRA could be drawn into meeting them head-on. This was the cleanup part of the action.

Fallon was herded into a group of about thirty men. He knew many of them casually and some of them well and he was not aware that any of those he knew were in the IRA, though a lot of them were, like him, more or less sympathetic to one wing or the other because it was the IRA that was finally standing up for Catholic rights.

The woman was let go and the wounded man was driven away in an Army car. The others were double-timed some three hundred yards to Little James Street where they were made to pass

139

through a gauntlet of paratroopers and beaten with short yellow hoses before they were loaded onto a truck.

The floor of the truck had been laid with triangular pointed irons and the men stood awkwardly on the irons and leaned against the sides of the truck or against each other and some of them crouched down and tried to brace themselves on the floor between the iron points. They waited on the truck for half an hour and then were driven to the barracks at Fort George, about a mile away, and when they were taken down from the truck they were made to run another gauntlet and beaten again, this time with rifle butts as well as rubber hoses.

One of the men was a young priest who was wearing a black sweater. He had protested several times during the roundup and afterward on the truck that he was a priest and a lecturer in philosophy at the University, and finally a paratroop sergeant said, "If you're a fucking priest, Paddy, where's your fucking collar then?" and he was marched into the big interrogation shed along with the rest.

Inside the shed they were made to line up four feet away from the wall and then lean forward, their legs spread, their arms wide and locked at the elbow, their weight resting against their fingertips. This was the standard search position, but nobody searched them and they were made to maintain their balance on their fingertips while the paratroopers walked up and down the line behind them, beating them with the short hoses and kicking their shins and stamping on their feet with the heels of their boots.

After the first few hours some of the men kept falling down and when they did they were kicked and dragged up and made to assume the search position at the wall again. "Would you tell us if you're IRA, Paddy?" *Whack.* "Do you think your wee terrorist mates give fuck all for you now, Paddy?" *Whack.* "You Fenian bastards are going to curse the fucking day you were born." *Whack.*

One corporal walked down the line behind them and ordered

140

them all to lower their heads and then another one came along and beat them for standing with their heads down. "Heads up, lads," he shouted, whipping at their ribs with his hose length. "Show a little bloody pride for fucking Ireland." A few minutes later the corporal who had ordered them to put their heads down came back and hit them for disobeying his orders.

When the paratroopers took their relief, some Coldstream Guards came in and a major ordered chairs for the men so they could sit down and rest. The major told several of the soldiers to go and get some electric heaters because it was night now and cold and there was no heating in the shed. Many of the men had cuts and bruises on their faces from being hit by the rubber hose lengths and a doctor went around and checked them to make sure that no one had yet been hurt badly enough to be hospitalized.

A half hour later the paratroopers returned and put them back up against the wall and it started again. One man refused to get up and told the corporal he was a sadist. The corporal called out to the other paratroopers, "I think we've got a real tough Paddy here. I think we've got a Paddy who is tough enough to be a member of that fabled IRA we've been hearing so much about." They dragged the man to his feet but instead of spread-eagling him against the wall, they forced him to lean over one of the electric heaters with his hands holding the back of the chair and his head hung low between his shoulders. When he tried to fight his face away from the heat, one of the paratroopers who was standing behind him crouched down and brought his fist up hard into the man's testicles and he went down and his head hit with a hollow sound against the concrete floor. A staff sergeant from the Coldstream Guards tried to interfere and told the paratrooper that for God's sake they didn't want anybody dying on them, but the paratrooper just gave him a look that said the Coldstream wasn't in charge of anything that night and turned away.

The man on the floor was groggy and curled in pain. He was a young man with dark wavy hair that fell over his ears and

141

around his collar and his face was blotched red from the heater. "I'm going to see if Gypsy Paddy wants a drink," one of the paratroopers said after a while. He squatted down solicitously by the young man and lifted him up by the shoulders and asked if he was thirsty. The young man nodded with his eyes still closed and the paratrooper told him to open his mouth. The young man opened his mouth and the paratrooper spat in it.

Gerry Fallon did not know what happened to the other truckloads of men who were rounded up that day. He said that the treatment of the group he had been brought in with was not particularly harsh when compared with what was often done to those who were lifted and interrogated. "They can really change a man for the rest of his days if they want to, youse know. We were lucky."

I was where all that had happened. I had put my fingers to deep saucerlike holes the bullets had left in the sides of the buildings and seen the black crosses painted on the pavements where people had died that day and I had stood in the wind by their graves in the City Cemetery. Their names were listed on an enamel memorial plaque mounted on the wall of the Rossville Flats and some soldier had battered a large portion of the plaque away with the butt of his rifle.

I wanted those deaths to matter, not just to the Irish Republican movement or the cause of civil rights, but to me. I had chosen them out of all the deaths there had been in that time and I wanted a connection between them and myself.

It was an accident that I was born Catholic, but knowing it was an accident did not change it. And it didn't change it that I said I didn't believe or that I thought the Church was an historical phenomenon that could be studied objectively in comparison with other religions, or that whatever it is that God is, He surely could be found in all the religions of the world and outside religion. I still sometimes stopped in at Catholic churches during the

142

day and stood in the back for a minute to watch the men and women who would be there honoring some private pledge they'd made or praying for a wayward child or an alcoholic husband; praying that it wasn't cancer; praying because it made them feel good, because it gave form to their lives and provided them with a way of being. It didn't matter that I thought they were praying in vain, or that they were misguided, or perhaps simple-minded or neurotic. There were misguided, simple-minded, neurotic people by the hundreds, by the thousands, and with vain hopes as well, walking by on the streets outside. I envied those who had the faith that I had lost.

I'd been in Protestant churches and they were always empty. Once standing under the great vaulted ceiling of one I remembered an article in a financial magazine about the power structure of American business. There was a graph in the article showing that 80 percent of the top positions in the leading corporations were predictably held by Protestants, and I'd resented seeing that word, *predictably,* in the caption above the graph and I thought, what do those Protestants who control American business have that is so great when nobody will visit their churches?

That was not enlightened thinking, of course, but it was a way of feeling, of giving focus to a resentment that had little to do with religion; that had to do with what, I wasn't sure. It was the way I'd felt that night looking out the window of the Council on Foreign Relations when the Irish Republican sympathizers had tried to set fire to the British flag. Well, the day had come when Harold Wilson had sat down across the table with the Provisional IRA. It had taken four years and by that time he was no longer Prime Minister but the leader of the loyal opposition lending his good offices to the effort to settle a bad situation, and the men he had to acknowledge, finally, were harder men by far than those who had demonstrated so ineffectually against him that night in New York, but their cause was the same.

But why should Protestants be the adversaries in the bottom

143

reaches of my mind? They had never done anything to me. They had not denied me a place in their world or closed their doors to my aspirations. I'd heard the old stories of discrimination, but I could remember no slights to my person because I'd been Catholic, and certainly, with my name, none because I was Irish. Most of the close friends of my life had been Protestant; only a very few were Catholic, and of them, only Eamon Brennan, the one-time candidate priest, had cared about his faith in any special way.

It was unfair, then, and more than that, stupid, to resent a past I hadn't lived when I shared so much with men who were like me in every way except for this sometime-Catholic thing they didn't know and that in a subtle way set me apart from them, so that for all our sharing, I felt myself different from what they were.

So what did that have to do with the Catholic poor of Derry? Their frustrations and angers were real and based on poverty and unemployment and humiliations I had never known. They weren't fighting over the concept of the Transubstantiation. This was no holy war. It had come about because to many Protestants in Northern Ireland Catholic meant being Irish, not British. Catholic meant Rome rule and no birth control and breeding like rabbits; meant boozing and unreliable and dirty and ignorant and superstitious. It meant what *nigger* and *spic* meant in America.

What happened Bloody Sunday was only an incident in a chain of incidents in a continuing civil strife. The Catholic poor had risen and disturbed the state and the state had taken off its kid gloves and retaliated. There had been riots and bombings for two and a half years and the state had said, "We will not tolerate their lawlessness any longer. We will show them our power and punish them." That's what it was about: the exasperated anger of those who had power and the frustrated anger of those who did not.

Thirteen were killed and fifteen were wounded. It was news on

144

the front pages for several days and there was great indignation and outrage. There were Irish demonstrations in many cities of the world and in Dublin a mob congregated outside the British Embassy and sang "We Shall Overcome" and burned the embassy down. Lord Widgery, the Lord Chief Justice of England, conducted an investigation and the paratroopers were exonerated because they said they had shot only gunmen and nail-bomb throwers. Then there was an unofficial investigation of the findings of the first investigation and months later, when it was already summer, there was a press conference to announce that the paratroopers had lied, but it didn't matter. It made for a story in the newspaper the next day but not many people read it. Too many other things had happened in the world and Bloody Sunday was old news.

By the time I got to Derry more than a year had passed and hundreds more had died on both sides. The deaths didn't have to do with me or my idea of Ireland or my Catholic past, but still I went to Mass in Derry, and not as an observer standing in the back. I went because of what had been done to Catholics there and to acknowledge that I was Catholic too. It was an irrational country and an irrational war, so I went irrationally. It wasn't Sunday but a Friday morning, and I did it for myself. Peter was off somewhere showing a brochure about a new kind of American industrial explosive to Joe Maguire, Irene's IRA brother, and while he was doing that, making his offer to be of further service to those who were doing the fighting, I was in St. Eugene's Cathedral up on the hill overlooking the Bogside, saying the prayers of the Mass that I hadn't said for years.

four

Peter and I waited for Joe Maguire at the Grandstand and kidded with the two young girls who were working behind the bar. Maguire was to meet us by nine and if he wasn't there by then, he wasn't coming and we were to go on to Donegal without him.

Peter said Joe Maguire was on the run again. That is one of the favored phrases among people with Republican sympathies. Just those three short words, *on the run,* and a man was identified with all the Irish rebels who had ever been hunted by the forces of authority. It is one of those poetic pieces of vernacular that conveys more than it describes, like that catchall term for violence, *the gun.* "Those days are gone. Now it's the gun." I liked them both.

I'd not yet met Joe Maguire, though Peter had the morning I'd gone to Mass, when the Donegal trip had been set up. The plan was that we were taking Kathleen and Gerry Fallon over to Donegal to visit Peter's friend, Phil Shanahan, and Joe Maguire was going along as one of the party in order to get out of Derry and across the border.

Shanahan was supposed to be a real character and not to be missed, but I hadn't been that keen on a night drive to Donegal.

Now that Maguire was involved, though, I was looking forward to it, because of what he'd been through. Back in Boston, Irene had told us how the continuous high-pitched whine of compressed air from the noise machine had driven him almost crazy, but Kevin said other things were done to him that were just as bad and that he was one of those the Army had tied up with hoods over their heads and thrown out of a helicopter. The helicopter was only four feet off the ground and instead of falling to his death, as he expected, he had only broken his collarbone.

As a reader of books and newspapers, I accepted that such things were done and had always been done. They were among the many cruelties and immoral acts that could be argued were necessary under certain circumstances. The IRA argued that the circumstances made it necessary to set off bombs and shoot soldiers. There are almost always reasons. But Joe Maguire was Irene Sweeney's brother and the fact that he, a particular person, had been tortured, fascinated me.

Though I'd not met him, I had been to his house in Creggan with Kathleen and sat by the fire one afternoon in the small kitchen drinking and singing songs with his wife, Maureen. Two of his little girls had done the traditional Irish step dance for me, their arms close to their sides, their feet flying, and one of his little boys stood self-consciously at attention and sang "The Men Behind the Wire" in a squeaky voice. When the nun in school had asked the little boy why it was that Christ died, he'd answered: "To save Ireland."

There was still a girlish attractiveness to the wife, but there was also a tired forward leaning to her walk and her face was tired and her mouth, full-lipped though it was, had gone hard with a dispirited downward turn. Kathleen had kidded with her about her husband being so rarely home, telling her she was getting old and that she'd better watch herself because her man had probably found another woman. Maureen kidded back and said she sometimes wished it was a woman that was taking him away and not Ireland.

147

She made lettuce and egg sandwiches for us and tea and she and Kathleen sang rebel songs, Maureen in a fine soprano that made me remember the stories of my grandmother. One of the songs was a beautiful lilting old one about the girl who wears a tri-colored ribbon around her hat for the memory of her dead rebel lover. I'd heard it on records but the woman who was singing it sitting across the fire from me had been hospitalized twice for nervous disorders because her husband was a real Irish rebel and not one that existed only in the verses of a beautiful song.

The two barmaids had been asking us how long we were staying and did we like Derry and telling us there were better places than the Grandstand to go for fun. I said we didn't think there was that much fun to be had in Derry and the one I liked, a little blonde with a face framed by short straight hair held by a barette, said I'd be surprised. She looked like a college cheerleader from the 1950s and I told Peter I was never going to leave; that this young girl had stolen my heart away.

"Aren't youse frightened to be here?" the little one asked.

"We wouldn't have come if we were frightened," I said to impress her.

"Well, at least youse know most times when there'll be a gun battle in Derry. In Belfast it'll start like that," and she snapped her fingers. "The bullets are flying all around youse every day over there. Oh, that's the hard town, Belfast is."

The other one, a long-haired brunette, asked Peter what county he was from and he told her Tipp and she said she was through Tipperary once and that her sister was married and lived in Kilkenny and away from all the trouble.

"I committed my first mortal sin in Kilkenny," Peter said.

"Oh, we don't think that way any more," the brunette said. "Sure a sin is only a sin when youse think it is."

"My God, when I think of the times I used to be looking around for a priest who was deaf and dumb to go to confession to."

"I wouldn't bother," the brunette said.

148

"I can see I made a great mistake to leave Ireland. I thought we were a celibate race."

"We couldn't be all that celibate or none of us would be here to talk about it, now would we?"

The Grandstand was a long, one-story building that was set at a right angle to the street so that it split a block of rubble-filled lots. The front windows had been blown out and were covered over with sheets of plywood and there were plywood patchings over part of the wall and ceiling. The bar itself was a short one, made of a narrow plank covered over with wood-patterned contact. It was the first place we'd gone to the night we arrived with Terry Keyes. We had been sitting in the back lounge with a half dozen old men watching a beauty contest from England on the television when the owner shouted from the bar that the Army had called in a bomb scare. Everyone had grabbed their beers and money and emptied out the sliding side door and across the street. A truckload of soldiers was around the place already and three of them were over by Peter's car and it turned out that that was what the scare was about: Peter's rented car with its Southern plates and my guitar in its old case in the back seat.

"Jesus, you're not going to blow up the car on me, are you?" Peter had asked a corporal with a walkie-talkie strapped to his back.

"Is it yours, sir?" The corporal had been very polite. He was wearing the standard patrol outfit of jungle fatigues, flak jacket, and beret, and his face was smeared black. Peter told him it was and showed his identification papers and then the corporal spoke into his walkie-talkie: "Unknown vehicle identified. Owner present with papers in order. Object in back seat is a banjo."

That had been our big adventure in Derry and we told the two barmaids about it. They had heard about the scare, but they didn't know it was only a suspicious-looking car with a guitar in the back that had caused it. They thought the part about the "banjo" was rich.

I ordered another beer and watched the blonde girl draw it and

149

the memory of the night with Eddie Barton in New York came back to me. I had not gotten over that night and the experience of being nothing in his eyes. It should never have bothered me that much, but it did.

"You don't by any chance have a tough guy for a boy friend, do you?" I asked the little blonde when she set the beer down in front of me. "Or a brother or a father or an uncle who is a tough guy?"

She turned to Peter, giving me a mock puzzled shake of the head. "Whatever in the world is your man talking about now?"

"Give it another try for us, will you," Peter said, "and this time just put it in your own words."

"It's nothing. It's just that I don't want to offend any of the tough guys here in Derry." I was playing it for fun when she couldn't have been more than twenty and I was never going to see her again anyway.

"Sure and why would anybody be offended?"

"I don't know. They might think I was trying to steal you away to America."

"And don't think she wouldn't go," the brunette said.

"His wife would be delighted to make her acquaintance, I'm sure," Peter said.

We all laughed and the little blonde told me I was a funny man.

"Right. That's it exactly. That's how I want people to think of me. As a funny man."

That's when Joe Maguire came down the bar to us with his hands jammed into the pockets of a bulky green zippered jacket with a hood folded back at his neck. He was tall with wavy dark hair and a full cowboy-style moustache and half sideburns and he looked like one of those fashion ad illustrations you see in *Esquire:* the rugged male off to watch the football game or for a walk by the sea with the wind blowing. The jacket was cheap and it wasn't that new, and the brown corduroy trousers were worn thin at the knee, and the shoes were old black wing tips turned almost gray and with the creases cracking through, but the way he carried himself, and the moustache, and what I'd heard about

150

him, made him seem different than any of the others I'd met in Derry.

It was almost nine and we were on a timetable for whomever he was going to meet across the border, so Peter and I finished our beers and said goodbye to the girls and we went and picked up Gerry and Kathleen at the Flats. A shop was still open in Brandywell and I bought some chips and some grape soda and we headed out the Letterkenny road to Donegal across the border, Peter and me in front, the two men and Kathleen squeezed in the back.

Maguire said to cut the lights and sing some songs as we turned down the street to the Army checkpoint at Termabacca and for me to get my guitar case up a little higher between my knees so that the soldiers would know right off we were a party crowd. "And the two of youse make sure to breathe that lovely beer breath on them when they stop us."

It was that easy. Maguire gave us orders from the back seat with Kathleen hunched over on his lap so you could hardly see him and the five of us were singing and humming "Home On the Range" as we approached the barbed-wire barricade of the roadblock. All the Army did was give a look at Peter's rental papers and check the license plates and look in the window and pass us on through.

That was all there was to running Joe Maguire across the border. We dropped him off about forty minutes later in a darkened village with no more than half a dozen houses and a church to it. There was a kiss on the cheek goodbye to his sister and another handshake and an "All the best" to us, and he was gone. I stood a minute with Peter beside the car. The sky had never seemed so dark nor the stars so bright and close. It was as if we were standing beneath a huge black umbrella dotted with thousands of peepholes through to the sun. Joe Maguire had gone through a cow path in the hedgerow and disappeared into the blackness of a field. I had not spoken to him directly, except when we were introduced at the Grandstand. What would I have said? What are

151

they after you for? What jobs have you got planned? What's it like to have a rifle jammed up your rectum and be told your bowels are going to be blown out through your mouth? I don't think he even knew my name.

Later at Shanahan's place Peter told what had happened and Shanahan hunched his jacket collar up around his ears and looked wide-eyed around the room. "Sweet Jesus, Mary, and Joseph, and all the other saints, don't be telling me it's the Irish Republican Army you're running with these days. Not the Irish Republican Army that's outlawed North, South, East, West, and all points in between. Don't be telling that to a poor old regular communicant and God-fearing man besides." Then he straightened up with a whoop of laughter and danced a shuffle step.

I watched him playing the fool for us and thought of what we'd done. Driving Terry Keyes up from Dublin wasn't the same. He wasn't listed. He went back and forth all the time and that was just a courtesy to save him bus fare. Maguire was different. But it was a small thing nonetheless and I shouldn't make too much of it. I could tell about it for a while back home at a business lunch or over drinks after work, but I couldn't let myself believe it was important or daring. He could have gotten out of Derry any number of ways. We'd never really thought there'd be trouble and I was never scared the way I'd been the night the boys were shouting at the soldiers in the dark. For us it had been a chance to play at being involved and we never questioned taking it. Maybe that was foolish, but then it was a foolish thing to have come to Derry in the first place.

Still I was pleased we had done it and I thought of Eddie Barton again and of the need I still had to somehow make him know that I was not just a man who kidded his way from conversation to conversation at cocktail parties, kissing the wives on the side of the mouth and shaking hands with the husbands and clapping them on the shoulder. And in my mind I said to the memory of him, "Maybe it isn't much that I have done for Ireland, but at least I have helped to get a man across the border. At least I've given a hand to a man on the run."

Shanahan lived in one ground-floor room of a converted police barracks and in it there were four old straight-back chairs, a table covered by a piece of yellowing oilcloth, a coal stove, and a rumpled bed in the corner. What must have once been somebody's dining-room tablecloth was nailed across the two windows that faced the road and a three-year-old calendar with a big color picture of the New York skyline was tacked on the wall above the bed.

He was a character all right, like some court jester out of a child's storybook: a small, impish man with a mouth full of crooked teeth, gray hair that stood out from his head from running his fingers through it all the time, and the bleary blue eyes and phlegmy laugh of the heavy drinker. There was hardly a conversational exchange that he didn't punctuate or conclude with that laugh or a shuffle dance step.

Shanahan had come back to Ireland almost five years before with a great deal of money and it was almost all gone. He had made the money on the stock market because one of his rich customers had managed his savings for him and Peter asked him what the hell he'd done with it. "Christ, Phil, I thought you'd be living like a country squire and not in a rat trap like this. What ever happened to the money?"

"The good Lord might know, but I surely don't. I think I remember having a hell of a time, though." He laughed the laugh and went into his dance. "I bought drinks for the whole county, I know that. And some for the other counties as well." Then another laugh. "But what is life for if not to enjoy? It's a long time dead we'll all be."

That's the way it went. He sawed off a piece of rubber tire and put it in the stove to start a fire with and heated some water to drink with the whiskey and we sat in the straight-back chairs

153

and watched him perform. He told us jokes and sang snatches of songs and recited "The Cremation of Sam Magee" and the first verses of "The Hound of Heaven," which begins, "I fled Him, down the nights and down the days;/ I fled Him down the arches of the years;/ I fled Him down the labyrinthine ways/ Of my own mind . . .". He remembered, too, the old days in Boston for us, when he had all the celebrities and the bankers coming to his bar and was a great favorite of some of the bankers' wives as well, but that secretly, and it was impossible to see him act out his songs and his poems and his stories and not be moved or keep from smiling.

"But I didn't look like this then. I wasn't wearing an old suit that hadn't been changed for a month." He grabbed his lapels and made an important face like a small boy and threw his shoulders back. "I looked the gentleman meself in those days." He collapsed into laughter over that and coughed into a dirty handkerchief and said that was no role for an Irishman like him to be playing. "It was a good thing I got out of town before they found me out."

"I think there were some who were on to you before you left," Peter said.

"Maybe so. But they never turned me in." He shook his head, still coughing. "Ah, but they were the fine days all right. Still, the days we have now aren't all that bad, with a bit of fishing and a bit of talking with the neighbors, and with the likes of yourselves, and work to do if you're of a mind, and always a glass to warm your heart when it turns to sadness." He shook his head. "Sure if it wasn't for the booze, we'd have ruled the world, and that's as true a statement as I've ever made."

Kathleen asked him if he was ever married and he stroked his chin and pretended to think hard on the question. "Sure and if I was I don't remember, Miss."

"She couldn't have been much of a woman if youse were."

"And what woman would have the likes of me?"

"I know some that would think they were lucky."

"And you're a kind lady." His eyes were soft and he bent over her and held her hand between his own two dirty, black-nailed hands. "But I don't think you're as smart as I thought you were before you said a kind thing like that." He dropped his head to his chest and did the shuffle step.

At the door, Shanahan blessed us all for coming and he told me not to feel out of place because I was "to home" and gave me a pat on the back. He told me, too, not to make any quick judgments about the land of my forebears. "Ask your friends here. The one thing you've got to learn is that you could be living here a hundred years and not know what Ireland is about. It's an upside-down country, that's God's truth."

Out in the car, Kathleen said Shanahan was a dear man and that what he really needed was a woman to look after him.

"I can tell you he was a kind man to me when he had it and I didn't," Peter said. "There was a whole year of my life back when the kids were little that I wouldn't have made it through without him, and I owe him for it still. It's too bad your brother couldn't have stayed with us to meet him. It might have given him a lift."

"Not Joe. He wouldn't have five minutes for a man like that, with no commitments. Joe's very serious about Ireland, youse know. And your man's serious about nothing."

"I don't know," Peter said. "He's a clown and all but he knows a lot more than he lets on. He was a good man once and something happened."

five

It was a St. Patrick's night again and I was back in Dublin. It was a party like any in the suburbs of New York, except that a middle-aged, middle-class businessman was telling me that the Irish were a savage people underneath, and not to forget it; and that if it came to it, Belfast against Dublin, it would be the hell with business and he'd be in it.

Peter and I had come back from Derry early that evening and the man wanted me to know that he didn't think much of Derry as a center of rebellion.

"Listen, Derry's easy," he said. "Sure they've got some hard men there, but it's Belfast that's the rough town. I know Cork and Kerry and the others fought well against the Tans in the old times, but it started here in Dublin, and remember that. When it comes to fighting, it's the city man who learns quicker how to do the dirty trick."

He had a youngish, strong-jawed face and neatly combed thinning hair over a high forehead. He wore rimless glasses and a dark pin-striped suit and appeared to be a lawyer or a bank manager. Most of the women were in long dresses and the men wore suits and ties, except for two in dinner jackets and one in a blazer and ascot, and it was very pleasant and there was lots of laughter, and yet here was this man telling me that if it came to civil war, by God he'd welcome it.

"If you want my opinion," he said, "it's only going to be settled with blood. There is no other way. Let it really break open up there, or let the bastards start something in the South, and then you'll see it. We're just hibernating now because we've had a little prosperity. But don't be deceived just because we all have a telly and a fridge and a car in the driveway now."

I felt that I should say something in favor of talking things out sensibly and trying to find a peaceful solution. Maybe I was for the IRA, but I was almost certain that I was not going to risk my life for Ireland. I figured to be safe at home if civil war should come, so it was only fair that I speak in favor of enlightened self-interest finally saving the day.

"Enlightened self-interest? That's the last thing that could be said about an Ulster Protestant. I don't care how many centuries they've been here. They're settlers. That's our land. Either they move in with us or they get out."

"I don't know," I said. "Civil war would be a terrible thing. They've got a hundred thousand guns, I've heard."

"Sure they've got guns. They've been talking about those guns for almost four years. But how well do you think they could use them? Do you think they could sustain a fight like the IRA? They say they'd murder us." There was a pause before the last two words and then he spoke them slowly and in a low voice and with his strong jaw thrust forward. "They wouldn't."

We were drinking and maybe it was just the tough talk that sometimes goes with whiskey, yet certainly there was enough violence in Ireland's past to support what he was saying. The capacity for violence lurking beneath the pleasant Irish surface wasn't admirable, but it was something to take seriously. The anger, when it had showed itself, had counted for something; had demanded some kind of respect. When his wife came up to us and asked him for a cigarette, I excused myself and went to the

157

kitchen to get another drink, assuring him that I would be right back, as you do at a party, because I was very interested in what he was saying and wanted to hear more.

The kitchen was a large one and modernized in the American style and it was as full of people as the living room. The host of the party was one of Peter's friends from his college days in Dublin who had made some money buying land in the west of Ireland and selling it off to foreign industrial investors. He was a medium-sized man and very trim and flat in the stomach and he had his jacket off and was doing chin-ups on a ledge that extended over the pantry doorway. He was very proud that he could do more chin-ups than his two sons could and he was challenging all the other men in the kitchen to try to match him.

A bleached blonde woman, whom I had talked with earlier about books and plays, said that I had to try it like the rest or I couldn't have my drink. She had once been very attractive, and vain, too, I'm sure, but her face was now too heavily made up and giving way to age. Because I had responded to her talk of books and her quotations from them, we had become friendly very quickly. She had told me she was despondent about her age and about her marriage to a man she didn't like, much less love. She had told me, too, that she had twice tried to kill herself over love affairs with other men that had turned out badly and that she had all her life pursued things she couldn't have. "If I knew then what I know now, I would do it all again, and again, and again; I would do it all a hundred times again." The statement came from a play of Beckett's and she said it described her perfectly.

So to impress her, and for her looks that were going, and for the years when she would have had the pleasure of being the prettiest woman at the party, I accepted the challenge and went over to the pantry doorway, doubtful about what I could do, yet, like a boy, hopeful that I just might do reasonably well and willing enough to try.

The ledge faced outward into the room so that the hold on it was the reverse of the standard chinning hold. I managed to raise

158

myself three times, barely making the last one while the trim-bodied host in the tailored shirt, whose name was Charlie Doherty, and who had really been very gracious to me, a stranger and unexpected guest, was calling them off in a loud voice, prolonging the sound of each number to emphasize how little I was achieving with great difficulty.

My arms were trembling when I came down and the host shouldered me aside and jumped up and did another eight just to prove he could beat any of us with ease no matter how many times he was challenged. I went over to the table where the liquor was and the blonde woman gave me my drink and my hand was still shaking. Peter had come into the kitchen while I was hanging on the ledge over the pantry door and I told him I was lucky to be still standing instead of dead of a heart attack.

"I hardly got two," he said, patting his stomach. "That guy's a monkey. I can't understand it. He must practice all day long."

"The hell with him. I hate him. I'm only drinking his whiskey to be a good loser. Listen, you want to meet a real firebrand, there's one out in the living room who's for civil war tomorrow." I pointed through the doorway with my drink to the man in the rimless glasses who was talking to a group over by the piano. "He's for taking on Belfast before the night is out."

Both of us were seeing ourselves in a more important light now that we'd been to Derry and hung around with some of the real IRA there and Peter was full of new plans for raising money for guns. He went back into the living room to talk to the man who had said he would welcome civil war and I stayed in the kitchen by the liquor table with the woman.

"I suppose," she said, "if I'd been brought up properly, I'd be a bloody Republican like your friend, but I'm not. What I don't understand is what you're doing mixed up in it. You can't possibly care about the stolen kingdom of Ulster and all that rubbish the way some of these people do. Not with your skyscrapers and your air conditioning and your Cadillac cars and all your wide open spaces back in America."

I told her Peter was American, too, now, and doing better with the air conditioning and the Cadillac cars than I was, but that he had a real connection with it through his father and I didn't. "I don't know, when you come right down to it, what it is I'm doing here, except that I identify with your country. I like the idea of it. It's a foolish thing."

"We should be flattered then. What was it La Rochefoucauld said, "The man who lives without committing any follies is not so wise as he thinks?""

I'd never heard of La Rochefoucauld but I told her I liked to think that was true, though I had my doubts. I asked her if she knew the Yeats poem that starts, "I am of Ireland,/ And the Holy Land of Ireland,/ And time runs on, cried she."

"That's one of the 'Crazy Jane' poems."

"Well, that's appropriate, all right."

Across from us over in the pantryway another man was trying to chin himself on the ledge and Charlie Doherty was counting slowly and in a loud voice and everyone was laughing.

Standing in front of the sink in the hall bathroom under the stairs, I could hear the sounds of the party through the door and I remembered how Stan Novak used to say, "I think I'll go shed a tear for Ireland," whenever he was going to the latrine. That was back in the Army before Novak was shipped to Korea. He was Polish, not Irish, and it was a line he'd probably picked up in Catholic high school, like, "Take two, one for after church," whenever you'd ask him for a cigarette.

It had to be an Irishman who made it up, though, if only because so many parents and grandparents had told so many stories about poor old Ireland and all the indignities that had been inflicted on it throughout history; had told of the penal laws and the Famine with the million dead in the ditches; had sung so many sad songs of failed rebellions. "She's the most distressful country that ever yet was seen, For they're hangin' men and women there for the Wearin' of the Green." Always the boot in

160

the neck. And then finally someone with no respect in him, someone who didn't want to go through life being a victim or with a victim's heritage, someone with a bellyful of beer, probably, said he was going to shed the most appropriate tear of all into the toilet bowl. Someone had finally said, "Enough of poor old Ireland," and then it had become a smart-aleck line for high school kids and soldiers.

I looked at the reflection of my face in the mirror and thought how it wasn't all that different from those Army days with Novak and how remarkable it was that it had been seen as recently as twelve hours before in the streets of Derry and now it was being seen for the second consecutive St. Patrick's Day drinking in Dublin.

I was having a grand time, playing the American visitor to the hilt; talking about business opportunities and the Irish economic climate; talking civil war; talking about life in a literary manner with the bleached blonde woman, who, it had turned out, was quite rich and whose family had been members of the Protestant Ascendancy when there was such a thing in Dublin before the Rising. I had told my story of the Sligo oyster venture that I thought would make my fortune, and how the mark of the Irish Church was on Catholics all over America, and how St. Patrick's Day in New York was an extravaganza of unbelievable proportions compared to what went on in Ireland. I was having a grand time.

Back in the living room a group was singing around the piano. There was a break and Peter started to sing "The Shan Van Vocht," which told about the United Irishmen waiting for the French fleet to come to their aid in the Rebellion of 1798. It was not a very singable song and he didn't know the words that well and it died by the end of the first verse. Someone started "The Wild Rover," which was much better because it is the kind of song you can pretend to sing even when you're not sure of the words.

The man who was married to the bleached blonde woman was

161

standing beside us. He was a graduate of Trinity College, where the ancient *Book of Kells* is kept; a stocky man with an amused, superior manner. His wife had introduced us earlier and said we were both Republican enthusiasts, so he asked Peter if he was aware that while the Rebellion of 1798 was going on in the backwater of Ireland, Nelson was maneuvering his ships to a brilliant victory at the Battle of the Nile that altered the future of the world.

Peter told him he knew it was Ireland's misfortune to have lived on the rim of real history. He said he'd forgotten about the Battle of the Nile and that all he remembered about Nelson was the big pillar that used to stand in O'Connell Street, which had been a duplicate of the one in Trafalgar Square in London, and which an IRA bomber had blown up in 1966 to commemorate the fiftieth anniversary of Easter Week.

"You Yanks make me sick," the man said. "You go over to America and make all the money you can and then buy guns with it and send them over here to a bunch of felons to stir things up. We don't want the bloody Six Counties. Don't you realize that?"

Peter, who had gone to University College Dublin, a rival school, said, "Spoken like a true Trinity man," and finished the rest of his drink and just walked away and left us there at the piano.

"If there's one thing I can't stand it's these fools who think the IRA is something heroic," the Trinity man said to a man on the other side of me. "You'd think it took courage to drive a car with a bomb in it up to some building. A bloody mugger has more courage than that. At least if the mugger doesn't get his victim the first time he might have to face up to a fight."

"None of us want the bastards, you know," the other man said to me. "Neither Belfast *or* Derry. There's not a man here tonight, except one, and he's a moron, who cares about the mess they've got up there. We're businessmen. We want friendly relations with England. Not these bombers."

162

"Sinn Fein fools," somebody's wife said. "Madmen."

"The 1916 men are the worst thing that ever happened to Ireland," the Trinity man said. "With the tri-color on their coffins just because they carried a gun in Easter Week. What's that, fifty-six, fifty-seven years ago, almost."

"There can't be more than forty of them left," the other one said. "Let's hope they die soon."

"I really don't know that much about it," I told them. "It's very complicated, I know that."

"Complicated, my ass," the Trinity man said.

"Well there's a lot in what you say."

"You can be sure of that."

What could I say to dispute these men? It was their country. The values they represented had created whatever prosperity Ireland had achieved. They were reasonable, practical men who didn't want murder in the streets. They wanted to increase their profits and they wanted life to go smoothly and so did I. How could I tell them that Joe Maguire's suffering at the hands of British torturers impressed me more.

Most of the Joe Maguires of the IRA were committed to a Workers Republic of Ireland, and what did that have to do with these businessmen singing around a piano at a suburban house party? Or with me? The trouble in Northern Ireland wasn't because the Gaelic chieftains had been forced to bow down to the Tudors; it was because the Catholic poor had no work to do, no way to dignify themselves through their own labor. If there had been jobs for them on some factory line, there would have been no IRA fighting for the Six Counties. It wouldn't have mattered what flag was flying up there if there had been jobs and food on the table and some decent housing.

Those were the economics of it, anyway. That was the part that was a proper subject for textbooks and not what I really cared about. What mattered to me was the simple fact of conflict. The economics were secondary. What interested me was the idea that

163

those who counted for nothing, who were not taken seriously, had risen. I was for Catholics as outsiders. I was for Irish rebellion and the relevance of the past.

For all I knew, some relative of my father's, of mine, then, was on the *Mountjoy* when it broke through and raised the Siege of Londonderry. I could have had forebears fighting with King William at the Boyne, or even with Cromwell at Drogheda. It was possible. There were Presbyterians among them, and Baptists and Episcopalians. They could have been on the other side back in Ireland's history.

Maybe for someone like me, my father's family should never have left Tennessee. And he could have met my mother some other way than in New York and they could have settled there and I'd have grown up with a Southern accent around Memphis, maybe, and had the Mississippi River and jazz and the Confederate graves and the land my people had lived and died on for generations all around me. Tennessee and the South would have been different from growing up around New York. I could have been stirred every time they played "Dixie" and I never would have thought of Ireland then.

There were other places beside Ireland I could have gone to and been around the edge of adventure and had a sense of past, and it would have been interesting and exciting and I would perhaps have learned something, too, about the people who were suffering, and about myself. A lot of it was just that: the change of scene; the going off to a faraway country at a dangerous age. I was doing now what I should have done at twenty-two or twenty-four. But that it was Ireland made a difference.

What if I lived there? Say I got some job with an American firm with offices in Dublin and moved to Ireland with my family. What would I do? Befriend the Hanleys so that I could visit them and sit in the living room of their Rathgar house where my great-grandfather had lived as a boy before he went to sea? Would I seek out the survivors of 1916 and listen over whiskey to their old men's memories of Easter Week? Would I take courses

164

in Irish literature at night or learn the Gaelic that I had been indifferent to at college with the Brothers, the Gaelic that since the Treaty with England was written everywhere on street signs and government buildings and taught in schools from the earliest grades, as if the imposition of an old language on everyday life could make Ireland a foreign country once again?

So a lot of people wanted to be other than what they were, or wanted to find a reason to be proud of what they were, or wanted to find some way to relate the facts of their lives to a larger identity. Up in Derry they had wanted me to sing "Joe Hill" and the union songs of the Depression because they thought that world still existed in America and that I represented it with my guitar and my leather jacket. They wanted me to share with them the songs of the workers' struggle in America because they thought it reflected what was happening to them. "Give us 'The Union Maid' now, will youse?" I told them nobody sang those songs any more. They didn't want to believe that. "Go left and you'll always be right," is what they told me.

One Christmas when I was a boy I asked for a transfusion from a Mohawk. Before the Foreign Legion, before Kipling, before the deep water sailors in from Hong Kong, before all that, it had been Indians. I really thought that by asking for a transfusion from a Mohawk I would somehow make real the world of tepees and birchbark canoes that I was reading about in books.

Well, I had the Irish blood already, if there was such a thing. I didn't need any transfusion for that. To like Ireland and want to be Irish was harmless enough. After all the years of sameness living in the town where I was raised and working in New York and knowing so well those streets and big avenues, Ireland was my place to go to. But to think that I could ever run with the IRA was madness. There were people in it who would look through the likes of me as if I was a dirty window and it was important to remember that and not kid myself about it and think I could measure myself against them. They were a different breed from me, so let them be. Listening to "Kevin Barry" and taking it

165

seriously was enough. Everybody dies and almost never with any meaning or useful memory. So take "Kevin Barry" and all the other rebel songs and enjoy them and let it go at that.

The party went on all night and I didn't realize it was as late as it was until the Dohertys' twelve-year-old daughter came downstairs and said she was off to the seven o'clock if anyone was interested. I asked her how far the church was from the house.

"Two blocks that way and one block the other," she said, dipping her head left and right, her hands in her raincoat pockets.

Those of us who were left were sprawled out on sofas and chairs in the living room after coffee and eggs. We had been listening to a man in a blazer with a bandana around his neck talk about the priceless heritage of Irish art from the sixth to the eleventh century that nobody knew about or appreciated. I knew nothing about this real art of Ireland, nor about the beauty and importance of Dublin in the eighteenth century, when it was the seventh city of Christendom, and I was pleased to hear there was something of value that should be proclaimed to the world. But I was almost falling asleep and when the girl came in and asked if anyone was interested in going to Mass with her, I told her I was. I was no less Catholic than I'd been in Derry, I thought.

It was daylight outside and the birds were chirping and it was Ireland. People were sure to be sleeping up and down the block on a Sunday morning and here we'd been up all night and seen the new day come. In the front yard of the house across the street there was one of those incongruous clumps of palm trees you see around Dublin. I looked out of the window and most of the houses were white stucco with walls in front of them and wrought iron gates and several of them had palm trees in their front yards. It looked like a street in Beverly Hills. Suburban Dublin looked like California.

"What is this, the return of the prodigal son or something?" Peter asked from the couch. "Are you trying to make up for all

166

your many sins, past and present? At least you could go at a decent hour like noon or something."

"I'll be asleep at noon."

"Well, if you're coming, you'd better come now or we'll be late," the girl said.

I shook hands quickly with the guests who were left around the room, thanked Charlie Doherty and his wife for a grand party and told him to watch out for me if I ever was in Ireland again because I was going to practice my chinning, told Peter I'd see him back at the hotel, and twelve-year-old Diane Doherty and I went off together to the seven o'clock Mass.